Letters to Heaven

FROM CRISIS TO CHRIST

Heaven is real. Really real!

KEN HORN

The Story of a Grandfather's Love, Loss, and
Rediscovered Faith

ISBN 978-1-68570-822-1 (paperback)
ISBN 978-1-68570-824-5 (hardcover)
ISBN 978-1-68570-823-8 (digital)

Christian Faith Publishing
832 Park Avenue
Meadville, PA 16335
www.christianfaithpublishing.com

All Bible scripture is from King James Version (KJV)

Printed in the United States of America

To all first responders. With special thanks to our volunteer Frankenmuth firefighters and surrounding departments, our Frankenmuth police officers. A big hug and thank you to our friends at Mobile Medical Response (MMR) for their kindness, before and after. And of course, to our emergency room nurses and doctors.

The book is further dedicated to the loving Hispanic community, in and around Frankenmuth, which embraced our beautiful Ruth, and welcomed our Horn family to be a part of theirs.

And, of course to our work-families for their constant comfort and understanding.

*****

God sends forth His people to act as angels for each other. Our hearts recognize each of the angels He sent our way.

Contents

A Grandfather's Love

1

A Memory of You Popped Up

My Dearest Zellie,

A memory of you from two years ago popped up today on my Facebook timeline. You were having so much fun standing inside an empty cardboard box. The box was almost as big as you. Included in that array of photos was a video of Liam trying to get inside the box to be with you.

You wanted no part of your brother joining you, and you stood your ground. Always confident, you even included an angry brow when needed, and otherwise seemed to get everything you wanted from your Opa. So on this day, I went into the garage and grabbed another empty box. Liam was just as happy with that one. Problem solved.

Zellie-belly, it's been well over a year since you had to leave early. It still hurts to write. Your Opa misses you so very much.

A friend came into my office yesterday, and we talked about you. He said he wasn't sure how his own daughter started reading my letters to you, but they had an impact on her. He said she kind of took a break from God, but our letters began to reopen the door for her. I knew what she was going through.

I took a break from God too. Until, of course, you happened to me.

Growing up, I was never very good at reading Scripture. Even today, with a study guide, I have trouble figuring out the Bible. I realize now how weak and imperfect my faith was, and that belief was shaken to the core when you left. It took some time, but thinking of you sitting in the lap of Jesus was the one thing that kept me sane.

Honey, it was you who introduced me to God again. You were like, "Jesus, this is my Opa. Opa, this is God!"

Sweetie pie, all those letters I wrote to you brought me to tears again. Every single one of them. Today's letter is no exception. The tearful mist of writing brings both joy and pain. The waves of grief crash again. There is no escaping them.

I write because not writing fills me with dread. I fear that I'll forget your beautiful face. And THAT I could never live with.

So many people have written to me saying how much our love, yours and mine, has affected their own lives. They felt how raw the hurt was and how deep the bond of love can be. Strangers feel like they know you through our letters as if you were their little angel too. From around the world, prayers went up.

I believe that because there were so many prayers for us, God just threw up His hands and told the Holy Spirit to show your Opa that things would be okay.

Because of the power of prayer, your Oma and I were gifted with visions from Heaven. Not everyone gets these gifts, I'm thinking. And I'm pretty sure you had a hand in it somehow. I picture your brow scrunched up, and you were giving Jesus a whole bunch of what-for. The relationship I now have with God today is not just faith. It is knowing that faith is real. A family relationship. A genuine gift indeed.

So, Zellie-belly, I've compiled our letters. I want the world to know how full of life and love you were and just how precious you are to me.

I will always love you more than the world is round — forever,
Your Opa

Zelda Rowan Horn-Grefa

I'm not a professional writer. I never had an inkling that I would be sharing my granddaughter's story as a book. A few years later, talking about my little girl is still hard. I am so grateful that I journaled our short time together with photos and letters, which you will find throughout this book. What I'm sharing with you is a story of both a grandfather's love and loss.

As Zellie grew, my pile of letters to her grew as well. I shared these letters to Zellie with friends and family through social media. People joked that Zellie had become one of the world's most famous grandkids. People asked about her everywhere I went. In a genuine sense, she became the object of affection of other people's families all around the globe.

As time went on, and after Zellie left us early, many people encouraged me to chronicle our love story in book form to share with other grieving families. The hardest part of starting was that while the letters had already been written, I had to reopen each one to tell our story.

These letters reminded me of the raw sting of loss, and it forced me to write through the worst of my emotions. It was hard to see the pages, which I stared at through my tears. It required hours of self-editing.

It pained me to think about taking words away from Zellie's story. Every moment, and every stray thought of my granddaughter, was right there in front of me. Taking away photos and words would be a little like losing her all over again, only by small pieces at a time.

*****

For those of us suffering a tragic loss in life, we often feel like members of an exclusive, awful-to-be-part-of club. Over time, we learn how to talk to each other. We learn when to be silent with each other. Some of us are horribly angry with God after a tragedy. Many of us find Him again.

Through it all, and with the miracles I have witnessed since Zellie, my faith has been restored. I know with all certainty that Heaven is real. Really real.

I've come to learn that yesterday is just a lesson to be learned, today is a precious gift, and tomorrow has never been promised to any of us. Make every moment with your loved one's count here on earth while it still matters.

2

Welcome to the World

Dear Zelda Rowan Horn (7 lbs. 2 oz.):

Welcome to the world! More importantly, welcome to the family! Opa and Oma have been waiting patiently for you and can't wait to get you home.

> *Your big brother, Liam, will show you to your room and probably give you a few tips on making your way around the house. You'll just LOVE our puppy Riley, and Riley will simply ADORE you! :)*

> *Be sweet to your mother. She just went through heck to bring you safely into this world. Hug her tight for us until we can visit her room.*

> *Tell your dad that I'm awfully proud. I can hardly type through the mist covering my desk area here. Oh, and let him know I've already picked out a nickname for you.*

With a hug as big as the world,
Your Opa

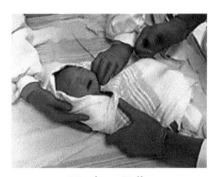

Newborn Zellie

PS. Hey, Zellie, I know your dad got little sleep last night, so you need to remind him to get some good pictures for our memory book, especially one with Oma.

I wrote my first letter to Zellie moments after we received our first delivery room photo. I had to work that day but kept very close track of my new little granddaughter with the big "owl eyes."

I had gotten into the habit of writing letters to my grandson Liam. Liam was born in Ecuador where my son Kevin met and married a beautiful young lady named Ruth. I welcomed Liam into the world, offering grandfatherly advice from a distance. The words in these letters are meant for the kids, but in a way, I am talking through them to Ruth and Kevin as well. In either regard, I signed off each letter with "Opa," being the German endearment for grandfather.

Back then, because of the distance and lack of traditional communications, Facebook and Facebook messaging were a reliable way to keep in touch with Kevin and Ruth in South America. When they left their village and went into the city, they could check in at an Internet café for an hour or so.

It didn't take long before my *Letters to Liam* became popular with our little circle of friends. The letters continued until Liam's arrival at the Detroit Metro Airport in the Summer of 2014.

Once he was home with us in Frankenmuth, the posts become known simply as *Livin' with Liam.* Photos of Liam were paired up with whatever conversation was taking place at the time.

When Kevin drove Ruth to the hospital in the wee hours of the morning, Veronica and I kept Liam home with us, and, of course, another *Livin' with Liam* post was created.

*****

This is how it worked with this post featuring Liam at breakfast. He is watching *Peppa Pig* on Oma's laptop as we prepare breakfast. To anyone reading the post though, it's made to look like Liam is running a sophisticated military-style command operation. This one we called "Operation Little Sister." In its own way, the Liam-at-breakfast post announced that something big was happening in the Horn household.

It wasn't long after breakfast that we had word that Operation Little Sis was a huge triumph. Zelda Rowan was born into this world; she was loud and healthy, and she was absolutely beautiful.

Livin' with Liam

Oma and Opa have breakfast duty this morning at command headquarters. Operation "Little Sister" commenced at approximately zero-dark-thirty! Hoo-rah!

Later that day, I had time to break away from work long enough to visit the hospital. Ruth was doing very well. Kevin was a proud father. Love hit me like a lightning bolt at my first sight of her. It was hard to put her back into her crib. Life had taken a beautiful turn. We couldn't wait to have her come home to live with us.

3

Opa's Little Girl

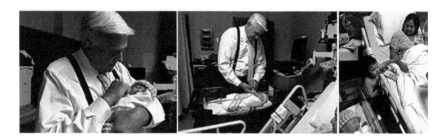

Dear Zellie,

The thrill of holding you today brought tears to my eyes. I hope one day you'll read this letter and know that you were the most loved baby in the world. It took less than a heartbeat for me to know that you'd be Opa's little girl.

Zellie-belly, when you leave the hospital, you'll be coming home to live with us. It's very early, sweetheart, but I'll make you this promise on behalf of your Oma and me; we will always strive to be the grandparents to you that my Opa and Oma were to me. My Opa was kind, patient, sometimes very firm, but he loved his grandchildren more than the world is round. My Oma, in her own way, was the same way. They were our protectors.

This letter I'll keep short because you need your beauty sleep. So happy birthday, little one.

With hugs as big as the world — forever,
Your Opa

I wrote this letter after my first visit with Zellie. I snuck away from work for this visit after three meetings in Lansing were canceled to get me to the hospital that afternoon. No one will ever remember the scheduling change, but considering the reason, I'm certain that they'd approve either way. To me, everything else in the world was unimportant.

As I arrived, Ruth was glowing but tired. Kevin was as proud as a peacock. And Veronica was making certain that the nurses and doctors were all doing their duties as I walked into the hospital room.

Seeing and holding Zellie for the first time was both the same and different from holding my two children. With my Kevin and Andrea, the world went into slow motion as they were born. I couldn't understand anything said in the delivery room; the doctor's and nurse's voices seemed muted and slow. For our new family, there was no one in the room except for me, Veronica, and the baby.

With Zellie, I wasn't there at the actual delivery, of course; but when we first met, it felt like it was just her and me in the room. I couldn't keep my eyes off of her newly opened owl eyes as she looked back at me. The world didn't go into slow motion, and voices were crystal clear. It's hard to explain to anyone that hasn't gone through it. But to those who have, I suppose no explanation is necessary.

A special bond is created when grandparents hold a newborn for the very first time. I'm convinced that the Holy Spirit is at work in that moment. That is when our souls become inseparable. It was a few years later that I began to understand the spiritual nature of that first touch.

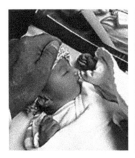

*****

When we left the hospital, Veronica and I stopped to get some Chinese takeout. As we finished our meal at home, I opened my fortune cookie. It read, "Something on four wheels will soon be a fun investment for you!" The next day, we went shopping for the perfect baby stroller.

4

Grandparent's Day

Dear Zellie,

It's Grandparent's Day today. I know it doesn't mean much to you now, but one day, we'll all be celebrating together. You and your brother are kind of a big deal around here.

Your papa and your aunt Drea never had a day like this. For a variety of reasons, they never had their grandparents around them. They just had their mom and dad. I was still new at being a dad. Believe me, I made my mistakes as a parent, which works out well for you.

Plus, with your big brother around us, we've already settled in as true grandparents. When we're babysitting, you'll discover that you'll have much more freedom to play and explore. When you're with Oma and

Opa, you'll be able to climb higher, splash in more mud puddles, and get food that tastes so much better.

One day, you'll be eating solid foods. You're going to love hot dogs with macaroni and cheese. Your papa might get a little upset like he did when he caught me feeding this to Liam. He thinks his kids should eat healthier. I explained to your dad that he used to eat mac and dogs as a kid, and he grew up big and strong.

When you're with me, you'll have fun digging dirt and stirring up ashes in the firepit like your brother does. Opa says have at it. Remember, though, your mother may not be totally fine with that idea. If she changes your clothes a few times a day, don't let that surprise you. Be patient with her. She only wants the best.

Finally, grandparents get a lot of leeway. So, Zellie-belly, on occasion you might get a little candy from your Opa. Like a Push-Pop from the hardware store. They have a small candy rack for good helpers whenever we do a project together.

You'll get to know Grandparent's Day. In the meantime, you'll always be Opa's little girl. I love you more than the world is round — forever,

Opa

In my early years, I lived with my grandparents, my Oma and Opa. I remember those days fondly. Days when my sisters, Heidi and Susie, and I would spend our summers playing outside. Most days we came in only for lunch and later when the streetlights came on.

Opa worked a full-time job and had a lawn-cutting business on the side. Oma spent the day making homemade bread, cleaning, and generally teaching us how to be kids. The lessons I learned being around my grandparents helped prepare me for life. I've lived my life trying to make them proud of me.

*****

My children didn't have the luxury of spending time with grandparents. Veronica's mother was at the hospital when Kevin was born. We have a photo of her in a hospital gown and cap holding our son for the first time. A month later, the day after Christmas, Marilyn was killed in a car accident. Our Andrea never got to meet her.

When I was just seven, my parents were divorced. For good reason, I wouldn't let my children meet the man who had become my stepfather. My mom was a very different person with this new man in her life. As long as they were together, I did not allow my mother to be around my kids. Kevin and Andrea only knew Ursula distantly in later years when they were nearly adults.

*****

My stepfather demonstrated true psychopathic behavior. He grew to be jealous of my real father. My dad moved away to Florida with his wife, Judy, when Bud threatened to kill him. Dad started his own landscape business in Pinellas Park and lived a modest life. My father and I grew far apart until years after he found his sobriety. One day, out of the blue, my dad called me from Florida.

Early on, I felt suspicious and cynical, thinking he was only calling because he needed something. The calls became more regular; first monthly, then weekly, and as trust built up, we grew closer than we had ever been.

He was born Joachim Horn. When he became an American citizen, he legally changed his name to Joe. Just Joe, he would say. My father moved back to Michigan and had a chance to get to know his grandchildren. Joe was a good man and died way too young at sixty-two years old.

*****

My kids' other grandfather was Leo. Our kids had a chance to spend time with him, but mostly on holidays. The times that he was with all his grandchildren, the kids had fun. Grandpa Leo would show them card tricks and would pull quarters out from behind their ears for them to keep.

Leo lived near us, but he had a life of his own that kept him busy. Everybody knew Leo. He loved being around people, and people sure loved being around him. He lived for polka music and spent time at German and Polish festivals in and around Frankenmuth.

Over the years, I believe that Leo never got over losing his Marilyn. I know he loved the heck out of his six kids. Even if he didn't say it, he was so very proud of the things they accomplished. Attended by hospice caregivers and surrounded by his children, Leo died of an aggressive bone cancer.

Whether or not we expect it, losing someone we love is always tough. Marilyn died instantly in a car accident; Leo died years later after a long battle with cancer. It seemed as if the biggest difference between losing mom and dad was the family's ability to say goodbye. Quiet goodbyes seem to bring closure.

*****

I tell you all this because I recognize how lucky I was growing up with my Oma and Opa. With Liam and Zellie living in our home, I felt like I had the chance to be the kind of grandfather that my Opa was to me.

When I mentioned in this Grandparent's Day letter that Liam liked to stir ashes in the firepit, I wasn't kidding. Liam was safe as he stirred the cold ashes, and it truly didn't bother me to see him get head-to-toe dirty. I didn't want Ruth to know, but down deep, I was actually kind of proud of him.

Zellie was the same as she grew; in fact, Zellie was so into ashes we ended up calling her Cinder-Zellie on occasion. This nickname you'll hear again.

5

Marking Time

Dear Grandkids,

As they open this time capsule, I just wanted to let you know how much your Opa misses you.

One of my reasons for running for public office is to make sure that Michigan stays a great place for you to live out your lives as well.

In either regard, no matter where you are in this ever-shrinking world, America, Germany, or Ecuador, I sure hope we've given you the tools you need to live successful, happy lives.

I truly hope that Michiganders are still eating lots of Frankenmuth chicken, the Great Lakes are still a pristine and beautiful sight, and I hope the Detroit Lions haven't gone another fifty years without a championship.

So…to Liam and Zellie Horn (and any other grandkids post-2015), I love you so much!

With hugs as big as the world,
Your Opa

They asked me to write this letter to the future to be added to a fifty-year time capsule in Lansing, and it is now buried with other items somewhere at the Michigan State Capitol building.

I wrote to Liam and Zellie, wishing I could see their expressions at the opening of the capsule. Of course, I'd be 106 years old by then. Sitting at my Senate desk, it never crossed my mind that Zellie would be gone from our lives so soon.

*****

The time capsule letter was a rare honor for me. But I recognize that it is important to capture everyday moments as well. It is essential to savor every minute with our children. While it is a good thing to look into the future, we should not hesitate to live in the present. And within the present, family traditions should be strong enough to withstand the test of time.

I discovered one of those simple traditions in measuring the height of our kids at every birthday. I wish I'd have been more consistent in measuring my own children, Kevin and Andrea. At the times, it occurred to me, I would measure them with their backs to their respective bedroom doors. But as we moved from one home to another, we lost those door-trim memories.

I had no intent on making that mistake with my grandkids. This time I designed and built a growth stick to be portable and able to measure grandkids at every birthday. You can see it starts out with Liam and Zellie but is ready to add more grand babies.

I started with a six-foot-long, one-by-six-inch pine board and traced out the lines and numbers. It took a couple of weekends to complete the project as I hand-carved and hand-painted all the lines and numbers along the board. The imperfections demonstrated my inexperience in woodcarving, but the flaws go unnoticed as we add our annual pencil marks.

*****

As I share my creations with the world, I play down the amount of work that goes along with it. In this way, I can add a little humor as you try to reckon with the "two-step" process.

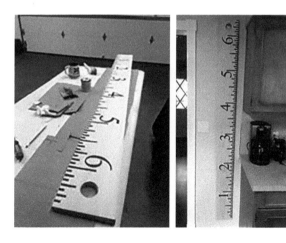

Another episode of Ken's Two-Step Do-it-Yourself Projects: This weekend, we're going to make a "Liam/Zellie Growth Stick"

Step 1. Remember what an elementary school ruler looks like.
Step 2. Make a fresh pine board look like THAT!

Two quick steps and—VOILÀ! If you have any trouble along the way, dial 1-800-CALL-OPA. :)

6

My Family

I cherish the memories and the relationship that I had with my grandparents. Being with them meant being home. After my parents divorced, my sisters and I viewed them as our actual parents and our true guardians.

I was about seven years old when my parents broke up the family. Heidi, Susie, and I didn't understand the meaning of divorce. How could we? All we knew was that our mother shoved us into the station wagon with a perfect stranger we'd never met before, and we were off on a two-and-a-half-year trip to California.

In an ironic twist of fate, this stranger's nickname was Bud. And Bud, as it turns out, was both an alcoholic and abusive. Physical abuse was common, but mental abuse and manipulation were more his specialties. My sisters and my mother received the worst of it.

My Oma and Opa immediately saw through his veneer. They loved their grandchildren so much that they followed us to the West Coast. They were a safe haven, our respite. We spent as much time as we could with my grandparents. Oma took us to the parks and the beach. Opa showed me how to roll up my sleeves to work in the dirt. I remember a day on a Santa Barbara pier, my Oma taught me how to run like the wind—back straight, with arms and legs pumping as I hit full stride.

Despite my grandparents' love and devotion, we still spent our days with Mom and Bud, flinching at every raised voice and raised hand. And we moved from rented apartment to rented house. From school to school, we moved. We didn't know the difference as kids. We didn't know we were dirt poor. And we didn't know they made the moves, always staying one step ahead of the current landlord.

At my best count, we moved thirteen times before I entered the sixth grade and three more times before I graduated high school. I came to hate the upheaval of moving. What destroyed me, though, was losing friends with every new location, with every new school. I would make a friend; lose a friend. It doesn't take long to learn that to avoid the pain; it was easier to be alone. I became a loner.

I felt even more alone when Oma and Opa moved back to Germany at Opa's retirement. Heidi left with my grandparents, and I felt like I lost her as well. Susie moved to Germany years later because of the horrible abuses of our stepfather. But in Germany, my sisters were safe. They were with Oma and Opa.

*****

I have another sister and brother through Mom and Bud's marriage. Ren grew up a tough, streetwise kid. Everything good in her life, she had to scratch and claw to get. Through sheer force of her will, Ren raised a beautiful family, stood by her husband when he nearly lost his life in a motorcycle accident, put herself through college, and ran a small business. Only God knows where all that strength came from.

My brother Buddy has a different story. Looking back, it seems to me, the quicker each one of us left the home of mom and Bud, the better off we were. Buddy stuck around the longest. He was always a great kid wanting to please. One of my sorrows from the past and one of my frustrations is that when I put up that barrier between my mother, Bud, and my children, I inadvertently put up a barrier with Buddy too. He needed a big brother, and I wasn't there for him.

*****

Seldom do I tell this story of growing up. I never want people to feel sorry for me. Life is too short to live with regret. I am exactly who I am today because of each experience in my life—good or bad.

Given a chance to go back and change anything in my past, I'd turn it down. Because changing even a fraction of a moment means

I would not have the marriage I do or have the kids I have. I would not have the chance at being the Opa I want to be.

I made a promise to myself and to Veronica to be married to her "'til death do us part" and that our children would finish school in the very same school district that they started in. You can see why this was so important to me. So far, I've kept both promises.

*****

Kevin and Andrea were both born premature. Kevin was six weeks early; Andrea, five weeks early. Kevin started out his first few weeks in intensive care, with his lungs not fully developed. He was diagnosed later with asthma. But Kevin grew up to be strong and healthy. While born early, Andrea was as healthy as could be, never seeming to even catch a cold.

Kevin was our athlete; Andrea was our artist. Both personalities were so different, yet they both had a great sense of humor. We had our moments at home as all families do, but there was always enough laughter to make it all worthwhile.

One memory of Kevin that often comes to mind is the day a friend offered to take the four of us up in his plane. Kevin was young and wanted to be an astronaut. We took off from the grass runway of the Frankenmuth Airport, the Wm. "Tiny" Zehnder Airfield to be precise. Once up in the air, flying over Saginaw and Frankenmuth at about five thousand feet, Kevin and Andrea both had a tight hold of anything they could possibly grab onto.

As we stepped out of the plane upon landing, our pilot asked Kevin, "So do you still want to be an astronaut?"

Kevin said, "Yeh, but I don't want to go THAT high!"

In that moment, he settled on wanting to be a ground control engineer with NASA instead. He later became an electrical engineer for Nexteer Automotive.

In the meantime, Kevin's high school sports career included being on a championship track team and state finals in soccer. Despite his asthma, he received an MVP in soccer as the top scorer, and his name is still on the wall of the high school as part of a record-setting relay team.

Andrea has a very quiet soul and always seemed to know her own mind. She knew what she liked and what she didn't. Andrea was born with a flash in her eyes that instantly reminded Veronica and me of Andrea's grandmother Marilyn. There was no mistaking the mood when you ruffled her feathers.

Quiet with a slow-fuse temper is an interesting combination, much to the chagrin of one elementary school bully, who constantly picked on Andrea. We learned from Mr. Everson during a parent/teacher conference that he was conveniently distracted as she finally got fed up. He said, "Why, it was just last week that your daughter rabbit-kicked the boy in the face when he wouldn't stop trying to pull her down off the monkey bars. Well, that's what I heard anyways."

Andrea never spoke of it. She didn't feel the need to. Andrea also didn't mention that she would be auditioning for Venner, the elite Frankenmuth high school choir. Heck, I did not even know she could sing. She never let us hear her practice. Veronica and I encouraged her canvas art and her piano, but her singing came as a complete surprise.

In fact, the first time we heard Andrea was at her solo debut. I don't remember the exact song, but I do remember shedding my first tears over her music. Where she found that in-tune kind of smooth-haunting style, I'll never know. She sure didn't inherit it from her parents.

As she continued to surprise us, Andrea decided one day that she was moving to Grand Rapids to make a life for herself. She's a hard worker and a loyal friend to the few people she lets into her life. And I miss our little girl.

7

Ruth

This book would not exist if Ruth hadn't found her way into our lives. Of course, we never expected Kevin to find his way to San Pueblo, Ecuador. He began exploring study-abroad programs. With a scholarship from Delta College and a student loan, Kevin signed up for a six-month program at Val Paraiso University in Chile.

Kevin was fluent in Spanish, having taken lessons since Mrs. Stricker's second-grade class and each school year after, including college classes. He was scheduled to be immersed in the university's program as well. After all, the classes would naturally be taught in Spanish, and he needed to keep up with the lessons.

We knew he'd be gone for some time as we said our goodbyes at Detroit Metro Airport. He was in excellent hands with his study-abroad team, and this was an opportunity of a lifetime. It was not long after our goodbyes when Veronica and I were startled one morning by a phone call from the study-abroad program leader.

"We just want to tell you that Kevin is safe," he said.

"Safe? What happened?" was Veronica's response.

"You didn't see the news? There was a major earthquake. It measured 8.8 on the Richter scale. We were all touring the City of Santiago, but the earthquake happened much farther south. Kevin is with our group. We moved everyone to a small resort farther up into the mountain. Again, he's safe."

Well, thank God! Literally!

It was a rocky start to Kevin's first trip to South America. Near the end of his time at Val Paraiso, we discovered that his six-month stay soon become a year-long journey, which would change all our lives. Once done with his studies, Kevin called home to inform us that while he still had six months left on his visa, he was going to hike and backpack South America.

He said, "This is something I just need to do. I don't want to look back and always wish that I did. I'm going to backpack my way across the continent."

With a few train and bus rides tossed in, backpacking is exactly what he did. On foot, he visited every nation of South America, except for Brazil. In Ecuador, he discovered an organic farm that was committed to replanting the rainforest. While helping with reforestation, he also taught English to children at a private school owned by the family of the farm where he boarded.

Ruth was a secretary at this school and knew no English. That didn't stop the two of them from falling in love at first sight. They grew to know each other's hearts. As Kevin's visa expired, he flew home to Michigan, knowing he would travel once again.

In Ecuador, in 2012, Ruth and Kevin were married. Veronica, Andrea, and I flew down that August to witness and celebrate the marriage. There are so many stories to tell about the difference in the cultures, the beauty of the land, the kindness of Ruth's family, and the people of the region. You can begin to imagine the pageantry of the young Quechua dancers, dressed in purples and other bright colors. Toward the end of their performance, they had a bit of fun including Veronica and me in their wedding dance.

When Ruth's father, Ricardo, raised a toast to the bride and groom, he spoke both in Spanish and in Quechua. The Quechua tribes of South America are indigenous to the region. Spanish settlers changed much in Ecuador, but the older culture is still very strong.

Because Ricardo toasted in two languages, I felt it important to do the same. I toasted first in English, which Kevin translated for reception guests. I then shifted to German, and Kevin joked he couldn't translate this *Alemán* toast. However, to me, it was important for Ruth's family to know that we have a rich history as well.

What they didn't know was that when Veronica and I unexpectedly broke out into song, the wedding toast song was actually a slowed-down version of the German beer-drinking toast, "Ein Prosit." Since my German was a little rusty, it seemed like a sensible way to end my speech.

Three of us flew back to the States, leaving Kevin behind to get things in order. We were counseled to begin the process of Ruth's immigration into the USA, on the American side, her destination. So when Kevin flew home alone, we began the arduous task of putting all the necessary information together. To be certain, we started out the right way; but any way you cut it, the legal immigration process is brutal.

Eighteen months later, with stacks of paperwork completed, thousands of dollars of attorney fees spent, and a nine-month-old Liam to pick up at the Detroit Metro Airport, we had Ruth here in Michigan. It was a fresh start with a new family.

The new family grew with our beautiful little Zellie in 2015.

8

The Furry Side of the Family

I sure can't forget to tell you about Riley and Bocephus. They are part of the Horn pack, and their names pop up occasionally in my letters to Zellie. Riley is our first furry friend. Her full name is Riley Cooper Bailey.

Yes, she has three names. We gathered forty of the most popular basset hound names, and with the entire family voting, those three names ended in a tie. Instead of having a contentious runoff vote, we decided all three names were just fine.

Riley was a rescue puppy. Her mother was rescued and had her litter at the adoption shelter. The mom was a beautiful tricolor basset hound, and they believe the father was a retriever. In a rescue situation, it's always tough to be sure. Riley has the short legs of a basset and the plumed tail and haunches of a retriever. She is mostly chestnut in color with a bit of black, and she has white socks. As with most rescues, she is the sweetest, most grateful friend you could imagine.

Getting ready for the big game

35

Riley is one year younger than Liam and was here when Zellie arrived. Both kids did their best to turn Riley into a miniature horse, trying to ride on her back. Patiently, Riley would stay still long enough for the kids to get into position, then she'd simply walk away leaving the kids standing bow-legged behind her.

*****

Bocephus came along about a year later. A full-blood basset hound, Bo was the same tricolor as Riley's mother. Veronica specifically wanted a basset and searched online until she found her perfect Bo. Inspired by country singer Hank Williams, Jr's nickname, and considering his southern heritage, Bocephus seemed the perfect name.

Riley watching over Bo on day one

And it wasn't just his name that made Bocephus unique. Bo was about as basset-ty as a basset can get, even tripping on his own puppy ears when he ran too fast. He grew to be a stout, eighty-pound cinder block. He had the deep bark of a big dog that could be rather intimidating if you walked up too quickly into his not-so-great line of sight.

*****

Both Riley and Bo loved to go for walks around the block. Going for a walk pretty much means going for a *sniff*. We'd stop at every tree, every hydrant, and every corner of a driveway where the homeowner put recycling at the curb. Reading the newspaper is what my sister Susie would call it. To Riley's lasting disappointment, Bo couldn't walk long distances. It just wasn't in him to do so. So in exchange for the shorter distance, we all agreed to take our sweet time along the way.

Riley became popular among our friends as they followed her escapades on social media. She even earned her own Facebook page titled *The Life of Riley*. Bo contributed quite often to the page as well. Anytime I was out and about, people would stop me and ask me how Riley and Bo were doing today.

Mostly, though, people knew our two world-famous pups because they saw them in photos with Liam and Zellie. We were all part of the same Horn pack. As you read the letters in this book, you'll see evidence of how tight the bonds were between the kids and the dogs.

*****

While Bocephus came into the world already named and loved by Veronica, he would become especially attached to Zellie. And Zellie always had a way with Bo.

Zellie with Bocephus

9

Never a Lump of Coal

My grandparents always made Christmas special for my sisters and me. With Oma and Opa, the entire month of December was magic. It started with the wonder of St. Nicholas, who would have been watching us all year round. This was the first test to see where we stood on Santa Claus's good and naughty list.

St. Nicholas' Day is December 6, a day when German custom has kids polishing up their best pair of shoes to place in the window. Oma and Opa would supervise us as we set about our tasks. We would all jump into our beds too excited and too worried to fall asleep right away. We were eager at the prospect of our first Christmas treats but worried that we might find a lump of coal instead.

Waking in the morning to a lump of coal in your shoe is a frightening prospect at any age. If St. Nick was upset with us, we couldn't imagine what Santa Claus would be thinking. As luck would have it, we always found treats: cookies, candies, and peppermint canes.

It was important, as a kid, to separate Santa Claus and St. Nicholas as two different characters, though the Saint inspired the story of Santa. Maybe because by doing so, we doubled the fun when Christmas was just around the corner.

With my grandparents, the tree always went up on time, new baking smells filled the house, and Sundays required the lighting of Advent candles as the wreathes sat on their own special table.

Waking up one morning after a fresh Christmas snow, Oma bundled us up, and Opa took us outside to show us the fresh tracks left behind by Santa Claus. Wow! How could one set of kids be so lucky as to spy the actual footprints of Santa himself? These memories are some of the Oma and Opa-type moments that bonded us so tightly to our grandparents.

*****

There's an old axiom in grown-up life that given time, people will never remember what you say, but they will always remember how you made them feel. With Oma and Opa, we always felt safe. We felt like we were important and that we belonged.

No matter what hardships we children faced after my parents split up, we still had the steadiness of our grandparents. This filled us with hopes of better days and kept us grounded and secure. That is how I hope my grandkids remember their Oma and Opa. We are so lucky to have them living with us to begin our own traditions.

Besides our own Horn holiday traditions, Zellie's first Christmas was made more special when the music director of Blessed Trinity Catholic Church asked if our six-month-old Zelda Rowan would portray the baby Jesus for our living nativity at midnight Mass. It was, as always, a beautiful musical Mass.

Zellie was the greatest baby Jesus ever. She remembered all her lines and remembered them loudly. The girl playing Mother Mary took it all in good humor, making it seem perfectly normal for baby Jesus to be crying during a church service. You'll read more about Zellie's acting debut in a later chapter.

*****

Between Christian holidays, Veronica is the driving force behind all things church related—from pew selection, to baptisms, to confirmations. Ruth is also church oriented while Kevin is not. Between Oma and Ruth, Liam receives regular religious instructions. Oma is the person as likely to drive Liam to catechism classes as she does for his piano lessons. In this arena, Oma becomes the steady rock.

I'm the one who teaches the kids to greet each morning with a hearty hello. Summer or winter, I would step outside with Zellie to say good morning to the trees and the birds. To me, there was nothing prettier than Zellie's smile as the first breeze tickled through her hair. She was as light as a feather in my arms, and it was always with a final dancing spin that would land her, three, two, one...into her highchair for her morning breakfast.

*****

As Zellie grew and learned to walk, she would follow her Opa everywhere he went. She would mimic every activity. By her second Christmas, at eighteen months old, she picked up a screwdriver to help me put together the "some assembly required" gifts that were opened. She would hold the screwdriver by the handle and touch the wood tray stand after watching me tighten screws. She was such a curious little girl.

One day, a fence gate closed behind me as I was walking to my car. Zellie was at that gate in a heartbeat, and with a voice that sounded like desperation, as she yelled, "Oba, Oba, Oba!" She got me to turn around and free her to join me on my trip to the local hardware. She was the happiest girl ever.

I can't tell you how big my heart felt inside my chest too. She was Opa's little girl, and no one could doubt it. It was my intent to encourage our budding carpenter. Among other gifts, Zellie would more likely find her own toolbox under the tree as I negotiated with both St. Nick and Santa Claus to be sure she'd never find a lump of coal in her Christmas stocking.

10

Summer of Content

Each year, as my birthday approaches on the calendar, Veronica inevitably asks the question, "What do you want for your birthday? And don't say you don't need anything! You always say you don't need anything."

Well, the honest-to-goodness truth is that I don't *need* anything. At my age, and after all the projects I've done around the house and the yard, I pretty much have any tool I need and know how to use.

I don't have any expensive hobbies that need annual technology upgrades, such as golf, hunting, and photography. When I close out the day, whether I'm home from my Lansing office or cleaning up from a home-improvement project, nothing beats sitting in the backyard with a good story to read and a fine cigar.

More to appease Veronica and our now-grown kids, I wrote a poem about being content with all I have. I started out working with a Night-Before-Christmas theme, which then somehow kind of drifted into Dr. Suess mode. But it got the idea across nicely enough.

'Twas the Week Before My Birthday

by Ken Horn

'Twas the week before my birthday, and all about the house
Every creature was stirring, including a mouse
Each chore on my list will be marked with a check
In hopes on my birthday, I'll relax on the deck

The children are out working or going to school
The grandkids require a crystal-clear pool
The puppies require both feeding and care
No time for a nap in the Lazy Boy chair

The screen door needs mending with rollers anew
Plus doggy proof mesh eager paws can't bust through
Up in the bedroom, the new drapes need hanging
Air conditioners need replacing, the old ones are banging

The bathtub needs caulking, the shower head leaks
Did I think it'd get better by waiting a few weeks?
The list keeps on growing, no time to be tired
Veronica's shoe rack is boxed, with "some assembly required"

The grill needs a rinsing to wash off the dust
The grate needs replacing, or the steaks taste like rust
I turn attention to the garden, in particular the lawn
The neighbors just love as I start up at dawn.

"On, weed and feed spreader! On, edger! On, self-propel mower!
On, weed trimmer! On, powerful Stihl Magnum leaf blower!"
After pruning the hedges, I turn my attention to flowers
Water them daily 'til we get thunder showers

Leaves and seeds seem to be blocking my roof gutter's drain
Ladder and buckets are needed, before heavy rains
Dogs digging holes now require a bath
Not enough hours in the day when I break down the math

Now... I look back on my week and it's hard to complain
I feel blessed in my life, as I'll try to explain
Wife and kids ask each year, what do you require?
For your birthday, what is it? What do you desire?

Nothing, I tell them, each year they implore
"Let me sit on the deck, just outside the back door"
You must want something *is the annual lament*
"I have everything I need, I am quite content"

I have every tool, which I need for the garden
And every gadget for my workshop, I'm beggin' your pardon
I own a car with a Hemi, I need nothing more
Than perhaps a touch-up for the scratch on the door

I don't need new golf clubs, the way that I play
I have plenty of ties to look sharp through the day
Of boats and toys, I need not a speck
Let's just cook up some burgers and sit out on the deck

Call over some friends and call the kids home
We'll sit on the deck, and make real this tome
We'll laugh and we'll joke, we can choose when we eat
I'm content with my life as I sit in this seat

So put aside gift ideas, settle in next to me
We'll celebrate the lives of our whole family tree
We will toast this day with a smile, until it all ends
"Happy birthday to me—on the deck with my friends!"

*****

So you get the idea; life is good and better with grandkids around. The summer of content included watching these kiddos grow. They truly develop personalities at each stage of life. Spending time at home on the deck was a lifestyle choice that I don't regret.

Even in the mornings as we stepped outside onto the deck, Zellie and I could take joy in simply strolling around the yard. We'd say good morning to the day. I was content to have Zellie in my arms.

As we walked the length of the fence line, she would watch for birds in the trees and hunt for other things to look at. All the while, she would have one hand reaching for bright flowers or leaves on the tree, with the other hand softly plucking at the collar of my shirt.

*****

As I began gathering my letters to Zellie for this book, I carefully sorted through all the photos I took of her. I logged pics of her as she had her first experience with an ice-cold Freezer Pop and photos of her eating spaghetti one-handed with her mostly unused spoon in the other.

Zellie would love to get inside empty spaces, and she'd climb up anything worth climbing. She was fearless and always knew what she wanted. Watching Zellie! This was my favorite hobby. She was large and in charge.

One morning as we were rinsing and filling the dog's water dish, Zellie pointed a tiny finger at the dish and commanded Bocephus to take a drink. In Spanish, she said, "Bo! Agua! Bo! Bo! Agua! Bo, agua! Bo! Bo! Bo!"

I said, "I don't think that Bocephus is thirsty quite yet."

But she was the boss of the dogs. So as Zelda leveled a stare at me, she turned back to Bo. "Bo! Agua!!!"

At this point, Bocephus kind of shrugged and walked over to the dish. He took a long drink of fresh, cool water, and Zelda gave him a satisfied nod.

Later that day as we were preparing supper, Zellie rolled into the kitchen on a hand-me-down, four-wheel scooter shaped like a Jeep. It was one that Liam had quickly outgrown. Oma handed Zellie a small dish of pecans from the pile she was sprinkling onto a pie. I noticed that Zellie was hand-feeding the dogs from the bowl sitting on the steering wheel of her Jeep.

"Zellie," I asked, "do you like pecans?"

"Yes!" she answered.

"Are you eating your pecans?"

"No!"

"Are you feeding your pecans to the dogs?"

"Yes!"

"Do the dogs like pecans?"

"No!"

Zellie loved sweet tomatoes and sour pickles equally. Like her mother, she loved the taste of Louisiana hot sauce. It just wasn't hot to her; rather, it tasted sweet. We'd never be surprised to find her quietly applying her mother's red lipstick to her face and arms in the morning. After a bath, she'd be just as likely to rub herself and her fresh white dress with ashes from the fireplace. I mentioned earlier that we sometimes called her Cinder-Zellie.

Thinking back on when our Kevin and Andrea left home, Veronica and I enjoyed life as empty nesters for about five minutes. Now, with a family of six, our home is hectic, rambunctious, and full of life. We love it. We wouldn't have it any other way.

*****

Zelda Rowan Horn was all full of sugar and spice and everything nice, but there was always a little vinegar waiting to come out too! And this is pretty much what everyday life is like in the Horn Household.

Every grandfather should have a little girl like this to love. I was content.

A Grandfather's Loss

11

Breathe! Just Breathe!

It was a beautiful summer Sunday. It was a not-a-cloud-in-the-sky kind of a day. It was a longstanding rule with my office that nothing went on my schedule after three o'clock in the afternoon on Sundays. I dedicated Sundays to family and friends with BBQs and time spent on the back deck. Sunday at the Horn's; it had come to be known. Seeing us outside, sitting poolside, as you passed by, friends would just shout out a hello and come through the gate. All were welcome to join us.

With that clear Sunday rule in place, it was highly unusual for me to accept an invitation from the NAACP to join them for their annual Freedom Celebration. The organization invites area legislators to spend an evening with their members. It's a time for people to get to know one another. I can't tell you why, but I felt obliged to accept the invite.

Knowing I had this dinner ahead of me though, I spent a little extra time with Liam and Zellie on the pool deck. It was a splendid chance to soak up some sun and watch the kids splash around in the water. Time flew by, and before we knew it, Mama was calling the kids in for snacks and a nap.

As Zellie came out of the water, she stood a few feet away from my lounge chair. She stood still, watching me watching her. It reminded me of a time I stood over my Opa as he napped, just to watch him. He opened his eyes twice then asked quietly in German, "Hast du etwas auf dem Herzen?" (Do you have something on your heart?)

I called Zellie over, and she climbed up and sat in front of me on the chair. Though she was only two years old, I asked her, "Honey, do you have something on your heart?" She sat quietly, leaned up against my chest. After some time, she simply got up and went into the house to find her mom. This is the image that later rolled through my head as we said goodbye to the kids and headed off to dinner.

*****

As we arrived at the Horizon Center, they asked me (as with other legislators) to sit on the dais along with the honored keynote speaker. They invited Veronica as well, but it was her plan to sit with friends at another table. They gave me a chance to say a few words before dinner was served. I shared with the crowd of about four hundred people that I've made it a point to never accept invitations to evening events on Sundays.

"While my office will politely turn down all Sunday invitations," I said, "I felt compelled to come here tonight for reasons I don't understand."

I went on to talk about how pleased I was to work with many of the great people in the room. I thanked them for the advice and kindness the organization's leaders have shown to me and my family over the past few decades. As I finished my remarks, I left the dais to join Veronica at her table.

We were just finishing our salad course as we got the first call. The look on my Veronica's face caused my heart to sink. She couldn't say anything; she could only listen. We left the building. She said, "Something's wrong. Zellie is hurt." I backed out of our parking spot so fast I hit a pillar. That memory is still etched into my back bumper.

We didn't know where to drive to: home or the hospital. When we received word that emergency vehicles were still arriving at our home, that's where we headed. While we were driving, Veronica translated a text written in Spanish. It was from Ruth. Veronica let out a wail that chilled me to the bone.

*****

Zellie snuck out the backdoor through the protective gate, and Ruth found her face down in the pool. The neighbors tell of a blood-curdling scream, which caused Kevin to run out of the house.

He jumped into the pool, pulled Zellie out, and performed CPR until help arrived.

*****

I tried to stay calm but drove much faster than I should have. Driving the short stretch of I-75 between Buena Vista and the Bridgeport exit, I looked down once to see a digital speedometer reading 130 mph.

Veronica and I arrived home to a sight that no parent or grandparent should ever be a witness to: Lights flashing, emergency vehicles of every stripe lined the street along our corner lot. They were still setting up temporary spotlights on the lawn where firefighters, police, and EMTs were standing and kneeling in a circle.

We could not see Zellie for all the first responders, but we knew she was there. I headed toward the circle of people when one of the volunteer firefighters, Stephanie Ittner, walked toward me to block my path. She appeared calm as she gently steered us through the gate to our backdoor.

*****

Inside, the living room and kitchen lights were off. The house was dark. I had the first look at my family, eerily lit only by the emergency lights coming through the picture window from outside. I counted heads as I scanned the room, and it led to the first glimpse of the upcoming and endless agony we would all face.

It was like that bad dream that you just can't wake up from. We all hoped beyond hope that someone would come in and tell us that Zellie's eyes were open and that she was going to be just fine.

In one corner, sitting on the stairs, Veronica was already comforting Liam. Liam was frightened and had his arms wrapped around himself. It was Oma's job to rock Liam in her arms and reassure him he would be okay. Veronica's sister JoAnn and our niece and nephew, KaLynn and Michael, were first on the scene. They all sat in stunned disbelief as JoAnn was trying to comfort Ruth. Laying at Ruth's feet, Kevin was a total wreck as you can imagine.

With the sound of the front door opening, Dr. Nettleman, our neighbor and family physician, walked in. I had a glimmer of hope. He said they still had a faint pulse and would prepare her for transport to the hospital. I asked about Zellie's brain waves. He answered, "We're taking one good sign at a time." That's when I knew. And that's when he asked me to drive our family to the emergency room.

Earlier, he'd heard the police scanner reporting a car ignoring red lights on State Street and speeding on the freeway. "Slow down and drive carefully," he said. "Don't be surprised if you see the ambulance pass you on your way there."

Ruth's friend, Mariana Barrios Shobbrook, came to take Liam for the night, and we began our slow trip to the hospital. As we were passing the Frankenmuth City limits, Veronica received a call from Aunt JoAnn asking if Zelda had been baptized. She was asking on behalf of Pastor Bender.

Pastor Gary Bender is retired from St. Lorenz Church in Frankenmuth. He was the Frankenmuth Fire department chaplain. Pastor Bender offered to perform the baptism so that we could be certain. In the car, Veronica asked Ruth and Kevin for their permission. Both nodded through their tears.

In an impromptu ceremony on the front lawn of our home, Aunt JoAnn, Cousin KaLynn, Cousin Michael, and his friend Serena knelt around our Zellie. JoAnn took Zellie's small hand into her own as Pastor Bender stood, Bible in hand, and baptized Zelda Rowan Horn-Grefa in the "Name of the Father, the Son, and the Holy Spirit."

Because he could think of nothing else to do, Pastor Bender baptized Zellie once more when he recognized that JoAnn just couldn't let go of her hand. She couldn't let go because she didn't want to. Finally, one of the first responders whispered, "We have to take her to the hospital. You need to let her go." As Zellie's hand was released, they all prayed together once more for God to bring her back to us.

*****

Back inside our car, aside from the sound of heart-wrenched sobbing, it was a very quiet ride. An ambulance did indeed pass us.

The timing was a bit suspect. I'm convinced to this day that it was a decoy to ease our hearts in some small way. This is why it didn't surprise me that Zellie wasn't there ahead of us.

They ushered our family into a quiet room on the emergency floor. Veronica was desperately calling our priest to help pray for us through this time. It was a weekend retreat for the Saginaw Diocese, leaving no active priests to answer our call. They were able, though, to send us a retired priest to pray with us.

When the emergency room doctor opened the door, none of us doubted what she was about to announce to us. Ruth fell to the floor as Kevin caught her and then kneeled next to her as she sat rocking back and forth in a chair. Veronica and I hugged and cried on each other's shoulders.

I looked up at the elderly priest who looked bewildered and out of place. He had been retired long enough that he simply wasn't prepared for this. He suddenly appeared very old. Even in the worst of my shock and grief, I felt a tinge of guilt for having him there with us. Not even a few minutes went by, and he stepped over to Ruth and started saying, "Now, now. Don't cry. You have to be strong for your family."

The hair went up on the back of my neck, but I reined in anger. I gently took hold of his arm as not to startle Ruth, and I said, "Father, now's not the time for that."

Veronica stepped in. "Thank you, Father, for praying with us. We'd like to be alone now. You're welcome to leave."

I thought he might be angry, but he had a look of relief in his eyes as he slipped out the door. Veronica knelt by Ruth's chair and held her tight. Kevin and I stood in the middle of the waiting room and hugged each other so tight. He asked, "What do I do now, Dad?"

Not knowing exactly what else to say, I whispered, "Breathe! Just breathe!"

It was the advice that I needed for myself as well.

*****

And now comes the part that caused me to delay writing this story for nearly three years. This is when they brought the four of us to visit Zellie in her emergency room bed.

There she was as the door to the room opened. Our beautiful Zellie.

Her skin was pale, but I was certain she was going to open her eyes, sit up, and reach out her arms to be picked up from her afternoon nap as she had so many times before.

Or that we would soon wake up, and this nightmare would end. It didn't end. Ruth crawled up into the bed, held her baby, and wailed. Veronica and I left her and Kevin to say their goodbyes as we waited in the hallway.

The hospital staff bent some rules to give us all the time we needed. The nurses protected Ruth and Kevin from the routine investigation that should already have taken place. They are my heroes to this day for that act of kindness.

When Veronica and I were invited back into the room, Ruth was sitting with Zellie on her lap, and Kevin was curled in a fetal position on the floor. Ruth asked if we wanted to hold Zellie to say our goodbyes. We both did.

It is the memory of holding the lifeless body of my little Zellie that stops my breath even to this day. It's one image in my mind that I can't unsee. This is the pivotal moment that invites the waves of grief to crash again and again. And…again!

12

Telling the World

Dear Friends,

This is the hardest thing I've ever done. I can barely read my own writing through my tears.

    Those who have followed the posts of my little Zellie know, without doubt, how tight she had me wrapped around her little finger.

    For those of you who came to know Opa and his Zellie through this page, I thank you for all your smiles and LOLs. We were all chillin' with Zellie. But now she's gone.

    Kevin and Ruth are so very private but were thrust into my public life. For their benefit, the funeral service for Zellie will be equally private.

    I appreciate all your prayers and words for my broken family. I love you all.

    For now, though…this is Opa…signing off for a little while.

    The day after, calls, texts, emails, and Facebook messages poured in. I couldn't respond to my friends and colleagues. I just physically and mentally couldn't. But I needed to make a public statement.

    Again, sitting at my desk, I stared at a blank screen through a mist of tears. I didn't know where to begin in writing a press release. I'd write a few words, and another wave of grief would crash over me. I'd rock back and forth in my desk chair, sobbing.

Each of us, everyone reading this story, has felt the sting of loss in our own lives. The grief we feel losing friends and loved ones plays itself out differently in every case and in every person. I was just shy of sixty years old, and I had never in my life felt pain this horrible.

It is excruciating. If time heals all wounds, I couldn't imagine how long this one is going to take. This pain came from a hundred different directions. Every time a wave crashed, it brought with it the wreckage of suffering, guilt, anger, and pain. And throughout the house, there was a drumbeat of sleepless sobbing and screams during the first night.

These sounds echoed in my head as I sat at my keyboard the following morning penning out a statement. My Chief of Staff Jami Des Chenes and Communications Director Melanie Rhine tidied up my words. I sent a letter first to my colleagues and then to the rest of the world to read.

NEWS RELEASE
SENATOR FOR THE 32ⁿᴰ DISTRICT
KEN HORN

P.O. Box 30036 | Lansing, MI 48909-7536 | Toll Free: 855-347-8032
senkhorn@senate.michigan.gov | www.SenatorKenHorn.com

Statement from Sen. Horn

LANSING, Mich. — State Sen. Ken Horn, R-Frankenmuth, issued the following statement:

"With a deeply broken heart, it falls on me to announce the drowning death of my granddaughter Zelda 'Zellie' Rowan Horn. Zellie just celebrated her second birthday. She is survived by her parents, Kevin and Ruth, and her brother Liam.

"Our entire family is struggling to come to grips with this tragedy and our first day without Zellie. Kevin and Ruth are extraordinarily private people that were thrust into a very public life. It is on their behalf we ask for space, and time to grieve.

"On behalf of the entire family, we would like to share our deep appreciation to our area first responders; firefighters, police and EMT that arrived quickly on the scene. We also extend our most sincere gratitude to the nurses and doctors at Covenant Hospital for your care and empathy.

"We thank all our friends and family, around the world, for all the love and prayers you've already shared. Please keep our family in your prayers as we struggle with this overwhelming grief.

"We will pass along details as they become available. Please contact my office for anything further."

###

Statement from Senator Horn

LANSING, Mich.—*State Sen. Ken Horn, R-Frankenmuth, issued the following statement:*

With a deeply broken heart, it falls on me to announce the drowning death of my granddaughter, Zelda 'Zellie' Rowan Horn. Zellie just celebrated her second birthday. She is survived by her parents, Kevin and Ruth, and her brother Liam.

Our entire family is struggling to come to grips with this tragedy and our first day without Zellie. Kevin and Ruth are extraordinarily private people that were thrust into a very public life. It is on their behalf we ask for space and time to grieve.

On behalf of the entire family, we would like to share our deep appreciation to our area first responders; firefighters, police, and EMT that arrived quickly on the scene. We also extend our most sincere gratitude to the nurses and doctors at Covenant Hospital for your care and empathy.

We thank all our friends and family around the world for all the love and prayers you've already shared. Please keep our family in your prayers as we struggle with this overwhelming grief.

We will pass along details as they become available. Please contact my office for anything further."

13

The Funeral

Dear Friends:

I did not intend for this to be such a lengthy letter, but those of you who know me well know that writing is therapeutic for me. I thank you ahead of time for indulging me these many words.

First, I can't begin to tell you how much you all mean to me and my family. It saddens me that it's impossible to respond directly to all your kind words.

Though I can't answer your notes, letters, and comments individually, I've soaked up every one of them and used them to gain the strength needed to be in the present with my family.

While you and I have this connection, Kevin and Ruth Horn are very private people. Both thrust into Veronica's and my public life. We've protected that privacy as best we could.

In their privacy, though, they were wondrously generous to Opa and Oma and our relationship with Liam and Zellie. Many of you watched Liam and Zellie grow up right here on Facebook through my Letters to Liam and our posts: Livin' with Liam and Chillin' with Zellie.

Together, we are all shocked and grieved at Zellie's death. I've never felt such pain and helplessness. Opa and Zellie-belly were a dynamic duo. Inseparable is the word that comes to mind.

Since Sunday night, this has not been a "one day at a time" moment for any of us. This has been a breath-to-breath struggle for the whole family, just remembering to breathe.

Thursday, as we said our last goodbyes to Zellie, we had two paths that we could have taken: a very public path or a private path. We chose the more private path because, again, that's who Kevin and Ruth are.

It was a very intimate, family-only service. Father Bob Byrne and Father Alberto Vargas led a beautiful Mass, both in English and in Spanish. The Homily focused on Matthew 19, where Jesus said, "Let the little children come to me and do not hinder them, for to such belongs the kingdom of Heaven."

Father Bob always paints a picture when he speaks. Imagine kids, he said, sitting in the lap of Jesus, pulling at his beard, and tugging at his ears. I smiled at the notion of Zellie sitting in the lap of Jesus and bossing him to give us peace. It's the thought that washes over me during the toughest moments. It eases my heart.

We privately broadcast the service through Skype to Ruth's family in Ecuador so that they could be a part of this ceremony. My family in Germany also attended the Mass this way.

Tomorrow, in churches throughout the Saginaw Diocese, in Michigan, and around the country, Hamburg, Germany, and Ecuador, people will pray for our little Zellie.

Isn't it heartwarming that this tiny two-year-old, in her own small way, is uniting people of the world? She's a once-in-a-lifetime gift of God.

On behalf of Veronica and me, we thank you from the bottom of our hearts. It means so much that you could share the joy that Zellie brought to us.

And on behalf of Kevin, Ruth, and Liam, please keep them in your hearts. They need you now more than ever.

To the thousands of people around our city, our state, our nation, and around the world, thank you for your thoughts and prayers. Every single one has helped.

If anyone wonders how the Horn Family will go on with our lives, well, I'm utterly convinced that our little Zellie is sitting on God's lap right now. With a scrunched-up brow, pointing her tiny finger down at us, saying, "Put peace into their hearts."

It's what she does. That's our Zellie.

Love,
Zellie's Opa

If saying goodbye at the hospital wasn't hard enough, planning a funeral was one of the most devastating experiences of all our lives. It made everything we tried to deny very real.

I could hear Kevin and Ruth crying nightly as I passed by their door on the way to my bedroom, where Veronica would already be curled up sleeplessly under the blanket. In the morning, getting up to prepare for our appointment at the funeral home, our grief ate deeper in our hearts. There were moments when we would simply walk up to each other and hug...and sob.

I had to keep reminding myself that as painful as it was for me, Kevin was still the grieving dad. The guilt he felt at not being able to protect his little girl when she needed it the most only multiplied his pain.

When his waves would crash, I would grab Kevin for a bear hug and whisper again, "Breathe. Just breathe."

*****

Caskets for a two-year-old are so small. We had to choose one. It fell on Veronica and me to make many of the decisions about where and when the funeral would take place. We would get a nod from Kevin and Ruth after Kevin translated our choices into Spanish. They chose the items that they wanted Zellie to be buried with, and Veronica and I ordered flowers for the church and the casket.

Guiding us through this process was Aaron Cederberg of Cederberg Funeral Homes. He is the consummate professional but was visibly shaken by this one. He took us step by step through all the details of the private visitation times, the church service, and the burial. The entire Cederberg family was so very generous with their hearts and the extra time they spent with all of us.

Near the end of the planning, we were forced to have an honest conversation over where Zellie would rest. We had no clue where Kevin's career choices would ultimately take his family. But we knew where Veronica and I would be in the end. We had previously ordered our burial plots in the new cemetery behind Blessed Trinity Catholic Church. We decided we would buy one more plot and that Zellie would rest between Oma and Opa. Picking a headstone could come later.

*****

It isn't a secret that funerals and burial plots are expensive. I know for certain that Aaron Cederberg didn't charge us fully for all the work that was done. Veronica and I were committed to helping in every way that we could.

But from out of nowhere, I got a phone call from a family friend, Debra Hardin. She was gentle and very kind as she described her group over the phone, *100 Women Who Care*, and she asked if she could pay us a visit.

100 Women Who Care meets quarterly to decide on a gift to a local charity. Members attending can propose a recipient for donations. They place these suggestions in a hat and draw three at the meeting. The chosen members have fifteen minutes to present their charity. Deb and I hadn't spoken in some time since Zellie passed, but when I asked if she'd share her memories for this book, she went into more detail.

She said, "Although I had been a member of the group for years, I had only once before submitted a giving suggestion. I had not planned on proposing one as I got to the meeting. Once there, I felt compelled to submit on behalf of Kevin and the Horn family.

"Our guidelines state that we give to registered charities, but I asked that we make an exception for your loss and the unimaginable pain you and your family were going through. I made my case, and a vote was taken. It was a unanimous decision to award the gift to Kevin and Ruth. It privileged me to be the messenger. The gift was given without strings attached or the traditional requirement to report back to the group as to how it was used.

"I hope in some way this gift was a blessing in the midst of such pain."

It was a blessing. Not only because it cast aside financial worries; it was another sign from the community that we were not alone in this crisis. And because Debra was the messenger, she spent some time talking to Kevin and Ruth. While the language barrier was tough to overcome with Ruth, Deb had known Kevin growing up as he spent time at her house with classmates. She talked about the pain she saw in him.

I asked her if she'd share that story with me as well. Here's what she said, "Yes, I only shared this with you today because I knew you all were in such pain, then. Coming into your home, you, Veronica, and Liam were so kind even during your own grieving.

"Because you're writing this book, I will also share that I have not been sheltered from seeing pain. I have lost loved ones. I've been with them at their passing. I've spoken with many people who are dealing with or have dealt with death, are coping with a loss, were victims of violence, survivors of suicide, or lost a house to fire.

"However, in your home, as I sat with Kevin and told him of the gift from this group of women, I have never seen such horrible pain as I saw in his eyes that day. I still weep as I recall his suffering. He will forever be in my prayers."

As I write about Kevin in this book, I recognize that he was the dad, and I'm just the granddad. But I did not capture his pain the way Debra Hardin just did.

I said to Deb that the family was so, so grateful for her kindness. And I said, "I'm convinced you had the Holy Spirit working in you through it all."

She had a very simple response, "I too believe I was a vessel that day."

*****

Planning the funeral Mass was no easier. Early on, there were two choices: We could make the funeral huge, which would require a new venue, or we could make it small and intimate for close friends and family only. We had so many people who wanted to show us comfort by attending a funeral. But again, it wasn't what Kevin and Ruth wanted.

Besides choosing the venue, Veronica was very sensitive to the fact that Ruth spoke very little English. Ruth would have felt helpless and alone if the Mass was spoken only in English. We needed to provide a funeral Mass in a language that Ruth could be a part of. So Veronica reached out to a friend, Father Alberto Vargas, to concelebrate the Mass in Spanish, while Fr. Bob Byrne repeated it in English.

We stumbled through the planning but still had so much to learn as we went along. We had not planned to allow for public visitation at the funeral home. It would surprise many people in the region to learn that Frankenmuth has a very rich and diverse Latino population, which wrapped its arms around Ruth and our family.

Gratefully, these friends of Ruth's just wouldn't hear of a closed funeral. So, there was Hispanic Wake. Friends Ivan Dominguez and Rosario Riojas and Juan Zarraga and Lupita Torres led the beautiful service, done both in Spanish and English.

The wake was also the first evening of a nine-day vigil, which encircled Ruth, Kevin, and Liam's grief. The novena shifted to our home each of the following nights. I learned the biggest lessons through this period of novena though I didn't make the connection until much later; grief is how you feel; it's a gut punch. Mourning is what you do; it is the painful first step into the grief journey.

While the time commitment made to this novenario is extraordinary, it does two huge very human things: it shows that we are not alone in our grief, and it actively transforms our grief into mourning. An important thing.

As we were prepared to say our goodbyes after the first night's wake, one of Ruth's friends shared with us that one thing missing was a floral headband for Zellie's hair. A friend who understood this simple custom explained it to Veronica and me in English. Now we needed to order the wreath prior to tomorrow's church service.

Headdress is not a common American custom, so our visit to the Frankenmuth Florist just a couple of days earlier didn't include this request. It was something that Ruth wanted but either couldn't convey in English to us, or in her grief, it merely slipped her mind.

In either regard, it's nice living in a small tight-knit community. From the funeral home at the edge of the open casket, I called Vita Hopp, the owner of the flower shop. We explained what we needed over the cell phone. Vita knew exactly what to do and worked overtime at the store to put together a dainty wreath, which matched the beautiful arrangements that already surrounded the casket.

Gene and Vita Hopp delivered Zellie's headband wreath prior to Blessed Trinity Church in plenty of time for the Mass. They handed the boxed wreath to Veronica, who in turn handed it to our daughter Andrea.

We were blessed to have our dear friends, Jan and Lou Conzelmann, fly up from Florida for the funeral. Both were a great comfort to Veronica and me when Jan agreed to help our daughter Ruth and Andrea set the headband wreath on Zellie's head. They all placed a hand on the wreath and, in this impromptu ceremony, together pinned the headband onto her hair.

It was perfect.

*****

We tried awfully hard to get Ruth's mother and her sister here from Ecuador. We wanted to have support for Ruth, who felt very alone. But we got little cooperation from immigration officials in either country, so we arranged a virtual Mass for distant families.

Ruth and her mother regularly communicated by Skype, so a dear friend, Gavin Goetz, who works for AT&T, helped us set up the equipment to broadcast the funeral to Ecuador and to Germany, where my family lives.

What our friends and family, at the church and living abroad, witnessed was a sad, solemn, beautifully prepared funeral Mass. Father Bob and Father Alberto led the service with such touching words of hope. I delivered some remarks about our little Zellie and was able to hold off the tears to the end of my eulogy.

What caught me off guard was Kevin's tribute to his daughter. He didn't say what he'd be talking about prior to that morning, but come to find out he didn't talk at all. He sang the most beautiful Scottish lament. I can't begin to tell you enough how this affected every person in the church that day. Zellie's death tormented Kevin in a way that we will never truly fathom, but he gave us a glimpse with his ballad to Zelda.

As the Mass ended, the pallbearers gathered at the front of the church to escort Zellie to her final resting spot. As they rolled the closed casket out of the door, it pulled the people of the church in its wake. We didn't have far to go as we walked slowly past the hearse and processed through the Blessed Trinity parking lot to the back where the cemetery waited for us.

As we reached the edge of the asphalt lot, the pallbearers carried Zellie over the grass to the carpet-lined gravesite. White folding chairs surrounded the small tent, which covered the casket as we lifted it onto the brass lowering device.

After a few more words from Father Bob Byrne, we placed single roses on the casket top as we began flowing back out of the cemetery area.

There was a very small reception for the immediate family at Aunt JoAnn's house. And then it was over. Well, that part of it was over. I felt so dead inside. Minutes turned to hours. Hours became days. Days turned into weeks. The out-of-body numbness felt endless.

We endured as life outside our home seemed to go on without us.

14

Returning to Work

Madam President:

While it's early and I still have the strength, I would request that my remarks be printed in the Journal as a tribute to a very special little Michigander.

To begin, while I've never been all that intrigued by Lansing politics, in a single heartbeat, political labels and petty bickering have lost all their meaning to me.

I've become more interested in all of you as friends and as real people.

My priorities in life have changed.

A week ago, Sunday night, my life became a breath-to-breath, moment-to-moment struggle, learning of the death of my two-year-old granddaughter Zelda Rowan Horn. My Zellie.

I've never experienced such pain and helplessness.

I literally had to remind myself to breathe.

Opa and his Zellie-belly were a dynamic duo.

Inseparable is the word that comes to mind.

Less than a week ago, on Thursday, we said our last goodbyes to Zellie.

It was a very intimate family-only service.

Father Bob Byrne and Father Alberto Vargas led the funeral Mass in both Spanish and English.

The homily focused on Matthew 19, where Jesus said, "Let the little children come to me and do not hinder them, for to such belongs the kingdom of Heaven."

Father Bob paints a picture when he speaks.

"Imagine kids," he said, "sitting in the lap of Jesus, tugging at his beard, pulling at his ears."

I smile at the notion of Zellie, sitting in the lap of Jesus, and bossing him into giving us peace.

It's the thought that washes over me during the toughest moments.

It eases my heart.

Madam President, this past Sunday, people prayed in churches throughout the Saginaw Diocese, all around Michigan, all about the country, in Hamburg, Germany, in Ecuador.

In her own little way, my tiny Zellie united people all around the world.

She's a once-in-a-lifetime gift of God.

Some of you might have followed our Chillin' with Zellie escapades on Facebook.

But as my office staff constantly reminds me, not everyone in the world is on social media.

So here's a small lesson in Zellie:

In her life-affirming two years, she handed us a million beautiful memories to recall.

With those memories, Zellie gave my family all the tools we need for us to fix our broken hearts.

Zellie was an angel. She was beautiful.

She had those rich, dark brown, almond-shaped eyes.

She was smart, funny; she was a little daredevil.

She climbed everything that needed climbing.

Zellie had to be rescued off the roof of our garden shed, again once off the outer walls of our backyard gazebo, and then off the rocket ship monkey bars on the beach at Caseville.

She wiggled when laughed.

Zellie was the boss of the dogs.

She would scrunch up her brow, point her tiny finger, and she'd issue a command.

She was persistent. They always listened.

She loved baby dill pickles.

She loved to dance. We have a video of Zellie twirling and clapping to Irish Step music.

We remember her laugh. It echoes in our hearts.

Zellie ran like the wind chugging along with her back straight, elbows up, knees lifted high.

She sang the alphabet song every morning at breakfast.

On our walks, she enjoyed hugging fire hydrants and cable boxes for some reason.

She constantly sprayed her own face with the garden hose as she opened the wrong end of the nozzle.

Yes, it was a very short two years.

But to Opa, every second…every moment is a precious memory.

On behalf of the Horn Family to all gathered both inside and outside of this Chamber, we thank you sincerely.

Your outpouring of support, love, and prayers is something that we'll always hold dear to us as we begin our path of coping with this loss.

It means so much to me at this moment to share with you some of the joy that Zellie brought to both Veronica and me.

And on behalf of my son Kevin, daughter-in-law Ruth, and grandson Liam, all living with us at home, please keep them in your hearts.

Father, mother, brother, they need us now more than ever.

If anyone wonders how the Horn Family will go on with our lives, I'm truly convinced that our little Zellie, right now, is sitting in the lap of God.

At the end of each session day, just before the Senate adjourns, members have a chance to express random thoughts and ideas under the Order of Statements. These remarks are duly printed into the official Legislative Journal. I prepared my tribute, and I prayed I could finish once I started.

As I wrote out this memorial statement, I had to remind myself that it would be the first time many of my colleagues would hear this message if they didn't read the press release or my Facebook letter.

Those who had, didn't seem to mind hearing my Zellie facts a second time.

*****

Early in this crisis, and during the worst of it, I took very few phone calls outside the family. Calls went to voicemail, even many of the numbers that I recognized. Not because I avoided my friends, but because I literally couldn't string an entire sentence together without breaking down.

I accepted calls from a couple of faith leaders, notably Bishop Joseph Cistone of the Saginaw Diocese and Pastor R. B. Ouellette from the First Baptist Church in Bridgeport. Bishop Cistone didn't know me nearly as well as he knew Veronica but gave me words of comfort on the call. I've known Pastor Ouellette for a long time. When he called, I didn't really need to speak. He called to pray with me.

A third call I took was from Senate Majority Leader Mike Shirkey. Mike is a dear friend, and I knew him to be a person of strong faith. He has a bunch of grandkids of his own. I took this call because he wouldn't place any judgment on me for sounding like a blubbering fool. My chief of staff, Jami Des Chenes, kept my colleagues up to date on my status, but speaking to Mike helped keep me stay connected and spiritually grounded to my work friends.

*****

When the funeral was behind us and as I returned to work, Senator Shirkey led a close group of colleagues into my office for a surprise welcoming. Our tight-knit group of eight freshman Republican lawmakers included Mike Shirkey, Jim Stamas, Wayne Schmidt, Margaret O'Brien, Pete McGregor, Dale Zorn, Marty Knollenberg, and me. They crowded into my office. We hugged, cried, and prayed.

As I entered the Senate Chamber, so many people came up to me to offer condolences and let me know they prayed for our family.

And there were those that shied away simply because they had no words and didn't know what to say at a time like this.

Three of my Democrat friends, which I'll remember the most, are Senators Mo Hood Jr., Curtis Hertel Jr., and Jim Ananich. Each never said a word. They didn't have to. They just grabbed me in a bear hug then walked back to their desks.

Sometimes, words aren't necessary.

A Grandfather's Rediscovered Faith

(the Letters)

15

Beginning the Journey

Dear God,

As this day comes to an end, let me say that I've always believed in you even if I didn't know it. On days when it feels like you're testing me, it's just me being a goof.

I will admit, though, knowing you're in charge of everything, it tickles me to think that my Zellie is going to have you wrapped around her tiny fingers, just like she did me.

Good luck saying, "No," to my little Zellie-belly.

With trust and faithful love,
Zellie's Opa

Writing this brief letter to God was not all that easy. While it appears somewhat light-hearted, it was still early in the grieving process when the hurt was still extraordinarily raw.

It was kind of like this when I almost lost Veronica after her emergency surgeries in 1995. We nearly lost our business during that same time because of time spent at the hospital and me playing Mr. Mom. Being strong and putting on a good face in front of the kids and in public is how Veronica and I tend to cope with stress. *Never let 'em see you sweat!* Right?

*****

Praying through all of life's obstacles and heartaches, I thought I was a man of true faith. After all, I was baptized and confirmed. I went to church on occasion. I knew the Lord's Prayer. Heck, I even tried to read the Bible a couple of times. I really did.

Looking back, it seems like all those fancy prayers were directionless. I'd pray, and those thoughts I sent up to Heaven, well, they just seemed to disperse into the atmosphere. My faith was superficial. And that is a hard thing to admit. At fifty-seven years old, and with Zellie leaving us, I found out the hard way that I didn't know squat about God.

*****

I was baptized and confirmed in the Lutheran faith at Cross of Christ Lutheran Church in Birmingham, Michigan. My Oma and Opa made sure that we went to church regularly. When my parents divorced, church became a distant memory, and the leather-bound German family Bible became nothing more than a knickknack collecting dust on the shelf.

Like so many before me, as a young man, I wondered who I was and why I existed in this world. Just like every other novice student of philosophy, I suppose. I'd have moments when I was sure there was a higher power and other times when I couldn't rationalize any truth beyond this life. The existence of God was just something to be debated among the most scholarly intellectuals.

*****

I met Veronica in 1981 when we both worked as servers at the famous Bavarian Inn Restaurant in Frankenmuth. Veronica had grown up in the Catholic faith. Though I didn't realize it at the time, meeting her began my slow journey back to faith. Her parents were devoted to their church and passed along that life's commitment to Veronica.

We married in the Lutheran church in 1983 after Veronica agreed to this conversion. After all, this was Frankenmuth, a community based on a rich German Lutheran missionary heritage. St. Lorenz is a stunningly beautiful church at the center of our community's history.

As I described, while raising our two children, Veronica was always our family's faith leader. Baptisms, confirmations, and organizing Sunday mornings were mom's job, and the kids knew it.

In 1988, as Andrea was born, we bought the Dead Creek Saloon located just outside Frankenmuth. At the business, we worked long hours for many years building up our kitchen and menu. I often worked seven days a week to turn this neighborhood bar into a family restaurant.

I grew our catering business and cooked under the tent at many of the community's festivals. On those Sundays when I was working, Veronica began taking the kids to Blessed Trinity Catholic Church. She enjoyed the smaller church community feeling within the congregation. It's what she grew up with.

On the Sundays that I could attend church, I still attended St. Lorenz. Sitting in a church on the other side of town, I thought, *Well this is kind of dumb, me sitting here with my family sitting in a different church.*

It took me until today to understand why it was so dumb. Church is an important part of a life of faith, but I didn't have a genuine relationship with God. Heck, I couldn't even claim a faith relationship with my family as I sat in a separate church on the other side of town.

*****

I started attending Blessed Trinity. There are subtle differences between a Lutheran service and a Catholic Mass. On the surface, two of the differences are the music and weekly communion. The

Blessed Trinity music comprised more upbeat music than I'd ever heard before.

It was the weekly communion, though, that had me considering a conversion. It was more about missing communion. I couldn't take the bread and the wine in the Catholic church yet. When the time came during Mass, I would stand and let my family out of our pew, and I'd sit right back down again.

Father Bill Taylor began teaching me the meaning of the Catholic faith. He saw my distress and put me through somewhat of an accelerated program. Weeks later, with Father's guidance, I became Catholic; confirmed in faith the same morning as my son. It was such a blessing to stand side-by-side with Kevin on that Sunday morning.

*****

In its own small way, taking part in Communion with my family made life feel more complete. But decades later, I found myself asking questions again. I had a great relationship with my family, but there was always something nagging at my spiritual side. Though I accepted His body and blood, I just didn't have a relationship with Jesus.

I didn't know how to build that relationship...until Zellie happened to me.

*****

Tragedies such as ours can tear families apart. Every part of life can become an absolute chaotic mess. I can't recall going through the seven stages of grief, but I watched as my family did.

One stage is anger. Anger drives us to point fingers of blame. If you blame your spouse, it might cause divorce. If you blame God, you may divorce Him. For me, I was not angry with God. Rather, the night of the accident when there was still a glimmer of hope, I tried to bargain with Him. It didn't work though.

Come to find out, the bargaining I was doing was my first foray into real honest-to-goodness prayer. And what I came to learn later was that while I didn't have a strong relationship with God, He had one with me.

Through the Holy Spirit, God has a relationship with all of us. So it didn't surprise me when He sent a friend my way to gift me with the daily devotional, *Jesus Calling*, written by Sarah Young. I surprised myself by reading it daily though. It helped.

That's when I began actively seeking stories of faith. I found the movie, *The Shack*. It was hard to watch at first because the story hit so close to home. It took me a half dozen times of starting and stopping the movie to get all the way through it. A movie and book that were easier to get through was *Heaven Is for Real*. Still today, the background on my smartphone is **Akiane Kramarik's** *Prince of Peace* portrait of Jesus that was described in the book.

You'll read more about some of the people that God sent my way later in this story. But I began recognizing that it was the Holy Spirit leading me down this wondrous path that brought me closer to Him. That's why my first letter to Heaven was directly to God Because I know now exactly where to find Zellie.

16

A Column of Smoke

My Dearest Zellie,

Honey, I miss you so much. You're still your Opa's little girl. There isn't a minute that goes by that you're not on my heart.

On my worst nights, the nights that I wept the hardest, I prayed really hard for a sign that you're okay. Well, I received my sign.

This week, something very strange and wondrous happened to your Oma and me that has me quite certain that you're in good hands.

I'm more convinced than ever that every person who experiences the loss of a child, or grandchild, no matter what age, can take great comfort in knowing that our kids are surely in Heaven and waiting patiently for us.

Because of you, sweetie, I can say without a doubt that all those small signs we experience are not merely coincidences. These small signs are real too.

I feel like it's only my earthly limitations that have me trying to justify the sound of the wind chimes we hung for you when there is no wind.

Or the times when I would hit a low point, and someone would write that their choir just practiced a song dedicated to you. Telephone calls, hugs, and Facebook messages all seemed to be timed out pretty darn good as I look back at it.

God sends forth His people to be angels for each other, and people are still showing up for all of us. Showing up for each of us grieving relatives who miss you so much.

Of course, I'm sure you've had a hand in it. The image of you sitting in the lap of Jesus has brought me great comfort as I've tried to cope with losing you.

Zellie, you had people all over the world shocked and saddened at what happened. I have to tell you that our neighbors, our town, and everywhere they knew you, people were so very generous with the thoughts and prayers they offered.

But now the picture of you sitting in His lap, bossing Him to put peace into our hearts just tickles the heck out of me. Just like your Opa used to do, I imagine Jesus must be rolling his eyes and sighing at your persistence. And that's when He sends his signs to us.

And the big sign I mentioned, I swear to you I wouldn't have believed this miracle if your Oma wasn't there with me. So as long as you're right there, tell God thank you from both of us. Because as you read this letter aloud with God, I want Him to know that I appreciate and love Him more than ever.

On your behalf, and through this letter to you, I also want to let Heaven know that in your two short years, you've made me a better person. Because of you, I'm stronger in my faith and feel that Opa's little girl is still a big part of our family.

You're still planted firmly in our hearts. And for now, as a family, we're asking Jesus to babysit you for a little while until we come home to Him. I sure hope He's up to it! LOL.

So, my Zellie-belly, if you don't mind, I might write to you occasionally just to let you know what's going on around here.

I'll love you more than the world is round — forever,
Your Opa

As I sent this letter out for the world to read, I knew it was more about me than Zellie. After all, at two years old, she would never understand most of the words I used. The letter wasn't grammatically perfect; none of them would be.

I wrote each of these letters to Heaven from the heart, usually in the morning, and always after some sort of inspiration through the night. Writing for me, as I stated, is therapeutic. Once a whisper of a letter entered my head, it wouldn't leave until I put it on paper. If this was the Holy Spirit at work inside me, I'm sure He wasn't asking for perfection; He just wanted me to get the job done.

The inspiration for this letter was the "strange and wondrous event" I mentioned. And I did not intend to spring this on you so early in this "Rediscovered Faith" section mostly for fear that you'd think this phenomenon impossible. That you'd simply close the book and walk away thinking, *Dang, this guy has lost his mind!* However, it's the first of three very real signs from Heaven that steered my footsteps on this new faith journey.

I blame no living person for their skepticism at hearing this story for the first time. I don't speak of this event often to avoid making people feel uncomfortable. In fact, my experiences from that evening would make me question it myself had Veronica and I not seen it together.

Heck, you should have witnessed the stone faces of the faith leaders as I shared my miracle. The few priests, ministers, or rabbis I've spoken to nod politely at me. I'm not sure what exactly I expected, but I'm quite certain they sat there thinking, *Listen, son, I've been in this business a long time. This just doesn't happen in this century. It's a great story, but…*

*****

You should know that while every single day after losing Zellie was unbearable, this day was particularly rough on the whole family. Veronica and I sat on the back deck, away from the kids. They didn't need to see us crying again too. Veronica was at the high-top patio table with her back to the kitchen of the house. I sat in the first chair to the left of her, facing west toward the pool.

There were no words left to be spoken at this point. You'd think by now we'd be fresh out of tears. It would be hard to tell we were praying, but we were. We were praying very hard with a lot of wishes tossed in as well. I hoped to hold my little girl one more time to say a proper goodbye.

I looked up, though, when the motion-activated light over the pool went on. Between the house and the pool, about ten or twelve feet up, appeared a disk of smoke. It appeared at a slight angle, with a diameter slightly bigger than a large manhole cover. It bent toward the ground as it grew forward. My unlikely first thought was of a jet engine exhaust. A presence of real energy. Quiet as a church mouse but exuding raw power.

"Smoke!" I said as I stood up. Worried, I took several steps toward the house to listen for the smoke detectors. I had no clue where this smoke was coming from. Veronica turned to see it and began a slow walk toward the growing column. Between the porch light and the pool light, we both got a better look at it.

As the column stretched down to touch the cement deck, it churned and rippled like a silky sheet of smoke. We've had a lot of fireplace fires that we've tended; this sure didn't act like any smoke we'd ever seen.

Mesmerized by it, I followed Veronica through the gate and toward this smoky pillar. It became transparent as we came closer. The nearer we got, the wispier it became until it was gone. It left no mark on the sidewalk. As we passed through where it used to be, there was the smell of fresh fire in the fireplace.

The first thought that came to both of us was that of our Cinder-Zellie. The girl who would always need a bath after stirring the ashes. After the column disappeared, Veronica kept walking in search of the source of smoke. I went into the house checking every level, touching all the closed doors for signs of heat. A second trip around the house yielded no natural explanation for the column of smoke we witnessed. Certainly not considering the power of it.

If you ask to this day, Veronica will tell you that the column moved toward her, not the other way around. She doesn't have a memory of walking in that direction, though I saw her and followed her. I feel like I understood the meaning of this vision while Veronica wondered over it for a day or two.

I called my sister Heidi in Germany almost immediately, forgetting the six-hour time difference. It was early in the morning there. It surprised me she didn't think her little brother had gone completely crazy. She understood right away that this was a real thing. She was the first to light a candle for Zellie and made me promise to do the same thing on my end.

*****

So was it real? Yes, without a doubt. I can't tell you why we were gifted with this sight, especially someone as broken as me—a man of such imperfect faith. But here it was—an answer to a prayer. Not the answer I was looking for, mind you, but the answer I needed. And boy did I need it.

From this evening on, I was no longer a doubting Thomas. All the miracles I heard about in church no longer had me skeptical. If this one was this real for me, there's no reason to believe I'd be the first kid on the block to see a miracle. Healing the lame and making the blind see were no longer just parables in the Bible. And the greatest miracle of all, the Resurrection, was real.

Now you see the inspiration for this first letter; the real and raw emotion behind it and all the letters to come. These days, when you hear me do an invocation or give words of comfort to grieving friends and I say simply, "Heaven is real. Really real!" you'll know where it started.

I know with all certainty that we'll see our loved ones again.

17

I Choose You

My Dearest Zellie,

Honey, I hope you don't mind that I woke you up a little early today. I had a good night's sleep and got up, thinking of you again. For the first time since you left us, my first waking thoughts of you brought a smile to me. A good feeling after all the weepy moments we've all had down here.

I know that occasionally you could get a little crabby in the morning. As we walked out onto the back deck, though, that first chilly breeze through your hair always put a little catch in your breath and brought the prettiest smile to your face.

We'd say good morning to the sun, the trees, and to the singing birds. Your owl eyes would hunt for interesting things to look at. By the time we walked around the backyard, your mama would have your breakfast ready. Before we opened the door to come back into the kitchen, we would do a couple of twirls and dance our way back inside for a 3...2...1... drop into your highchair.

The storm of grief hasn't ended. It's just that the crashing waves are further apart these days.

I still miss the heck out of you. But you know this, don't you? I know you're watching all of us, your mama and papa, your Oma and me, Liam, and all your aunts and uncles.

I've been doing a lot of praying and studying about this, and I've discovered that everyone grieves differently because the love we have for you is both unique and wonderful to each of us.

As for your Opa, people would tease me, saying that you had me wrapped around your little finger. It was certainly more than that. Not only did you pull on Opa's heartstrings, Zellie-belly, but you also had a pretty firm bear hug on my soul.

When I think about the grief we feel down here, it seems the tighter we hang on to each other, heart and soul, the harder it is to let go. A sudden death like yours is literally a blunt-force trauma to each of us left behind. The pain is very real.

And if given the choice between this real, physical agony and forgetting your beautiful face… I choose you. The pain I can live with.

I guess I didn't mean to get so serious on you, honey. It just seems to flow out of me as I write.

Today you made me smile. It gives me hope that more days like this one are ahead of us. You tugged my soul in your direction in Heaven and made me believe again. Ends up, you were a wiser old soul than your Opa.

I wish I would have paid more attention to the direction you were pulling me while you were here, but I realize now that I'm a better human being because of you being near me.

You prove to me that God doesn't make mistakes. You're perfect enough to be by His side, and I know for certain that with Him guiding me, someday we'll be twirling together on the deck once again.

Oh, and if they have vegetables in Heaven, be sure to eat every carrot and "pea" on your plate. Hey. I've got a million of 'em. ☺

I love you more than the world is round — forever,
Your Opa

A while back, I read that grief was like a shipwreck. You're hanging on for dear life on a broken timber. The waves are crashing over the top of your head while you suck in air in between the waves. In this letter, I talk about my crashing waves.

This shipwreck model of grief is something I learned from a friend who shared a simple question, which was posted on Riddick social media years ago.

As I read the question and then the response, I imagined the author to be hardened and weathered by the sea. Regardless of what this author may look like, the answer he gives here is epic.

*****

My Friend Just Died. I Don't Know What to Do.

Alright, here goes. I'm old. What that means is that I've survived (so far) and a lot of people I've known and loved did not. I've lost friends, best friends, acquaintances, co-workers, grandparents, mom, relatives, teachers, mentors, students, neighbors, and a host of other folks. I have no children, and I can't imagine the pain it must be to lose a child. But here's my two cents.

I wish I could say you get used to people dying. I never did. I don't want to. It tears a hole through me whenever somebody I love dies, no matter the circumstances. But I don't want it to "not matter." I don't want it to be something that just passes.

My scars are a testament to the love and the relationship that I had for and with that person. And if the scar is deep, so was the love. So be it. Scars are a testament to life. Scars are a testament that I can love deeply and live deeply and be cut, or even gouged, and that I can heal and continue to live and continue to love. And the scar tissue is stronger than the original flesh ever was. Scars are a testament to life. Scars are only ugly to people who can't see.

As for grief, you'll find it comes in waves. When the ship is first wrecked, you're drowning, with wreckage all around you. Everything floating around you reminds you of the beauty and the magnificence of the ship that was and is no more. And all you can do is float. You find some piece of the wreckage and you hang on for a while. Maybe it's some physical thing. Maybe it's a happy memory or a photograph. Maybe it's a person who is also floating. For a while, all you can do is float. Stay alive.

In the beginning, the waves are 100 feet tall and crash over you without mercy. They come 10 seconds apart and don't even give you time to catch your breath. All you can do is hang on and float. After a while, maybe weeks, maybe months, you'll find the waves are still 100 feet tall, but they come further apart. When they come, they still crash all over you and wipe you out.

But in between, you can breathe, you can function. You never know what's going to trigger the grief. It might be a song, a picture, a street intersection, the smell of a cup of coffee. It can be just about anything...and the wave comes crashing. But in between waves, there is life.

Somewhere down the line, and it's different for everybody, you find that the waves are only 80 feet tall. Or 50 feet tall. And while they still come, they come further apart. You can see them coming. An anniversary, a birthday, or Christmas, or landing at O'Hare. You can see it coming, for the most part, and prepare yourself. And when it washes over you, you know that somehow you will, again, come out the other side. Soaking wet, sputtering, still hanging on to some tiny piece of the wreckage, but you'll come out.

Take it from an old guy. The waves never stop coming, and somehow you don't really want them to. But you learn that you'll survive them. And other waves will come. And you'll survive them too. If you're lucky, you'll have lots of scars from lots of loves. And lots of shipwrecks. (Author unknown)

*****

The waves will come just as the old man described them, smaller and farther apart over time, but they'll show up to swallow you whole if you're unprepared. I've talked with so many people who had to come to grips with the reality that the waves never stop.

Indeed, my waves crashed at the most unexpected times; the way the wind blows through my hair as when I held Zellie on our walks, a certain song will come on the radio, or when I'm lying in bed, and sad thoughts sneak uninvited into my head.

I want to block it out, but I don't want to forget her face, her voice, our happiness together. This is the emotional trap we set for ourselves; we don't want to forget, so we wrap ourselves in memories. In turn, our best memories remind us of our horrible loss.

It's what inspired this letter to Heaven. I chose to remember to write it all down. I studied photos of Zellie and listened to her recorded voice. I dared the waves to crash down on me.

"And if given the choice between this real, physical agony and forgetting your beautiful face… I choose you. The pain I can live with."

The thing that got me through the worst of the agony was knowing that I wasn't alone. That we, Zellie and I, weren't alone. I know perfectly well that my vision of Zellie sitting in the lap of Jesus is a construct of my earthly vision of Heaven. But it comforts me and provides me with a deeper friendship with God.

In my head, seeing Jesus hold my little girl makes Him human once again. It takes the sting away.

18

Seeking Wisdom

My Dearest Zellie,

We just celebrated your mama's birthday yesterday. I know you were watching, but I promised that I'd keep writing to you to let you know how we're doing down here.

Birthdays aren't the same as they used to be. This one was a quiet, subdued celebration. Oma bought some cool candles for the cake though. I kept thinking about how big your eyes would have gotten as you watched the way they sparkled when lit.

We sang Happy Birthday and set the small cake in front of your mama. Liam blew out the candles alone this year but, as you can see in the video, he sure could have used your help. LOL.

Funny thing was that the photos from last year's birthday popped up as a Facebook memory today. Which, I suppose, is what got me thinking about this letter to you. You were sitting on your mama's lap for the party. You were just a baby back then and didn't know that candles even needed to be blown out. So, you watched Mama and Liam do it.

Honey, you and I talked about some signs that we're getting from Heaven and that I'm certain that you are right here with us. But with today's technology, your image can just pop up out of nothing, literally, to act as a sign.

When this happens, it can make your Opa sad and happy at the same time. I'll be forever in awe of the Zellie-belly that came into my life and rocked my soul to the core from the very first touch.

I catch glimpses of you and can only think, How in the Heavens could God have created such a beautiful little being as you? *I know, I know…the answer is obvious. He's God!*

Either way, as I look back on my imperfect faith, I can't help but wonder what God ever saw in me that made Him believe I could possibly deserve you. Blessings are miracles in every way.

Listen, sweetie, I'm wondering if you could do Opa a big favor? As long as you're right there with Jesus, would you let Him know that I get it now? I'm all in! I am humbled beyond all recognition these days.

If it looks like I'm just wandering around down here, seeking Wisdom, would you point down and remind Wisdom what I look like? She'd be a big help to your old Opa right about now.

In the meantime, make sure to give your mom and dad some big hugs. They miss you so much. With the holidays just around the corner, I know they would love to get a little extra squeeze around the neck and a kiss on the cheek.

I'll write again soon.

With more love than the world is round — forever,
Your Opa

One year prior to this letter, we were all together celebrating Ruth's birthday. For grown-ups, birthdays lose some of their importance. To children, however, birthdays are extraordinary things.

Ruth's birthday was more about Liam and Zellie than it was about Mama.

This year, though, to the grown-ups, Ruth's birthday was a painful exercise. I don't know how well we pulled it off, but we tried to bring some normalcy to Liam's life. Liam surely loves his mother and father, and he loved his sister Zellie too.

Liam stayed at Mariana's home on the days leading up to and just after the funeral. He complained our "house was too sad" for him. He didn't enjoy being around it. We packed clothes and toys to send along, and Liam had other boys to play with there.

But kids see everything! For good or bad, Liam watched how grief affected each of us. We could try to act normal, and acting is what we did. Ruth only agreed to this small birthday celebration for Liam's sake. Liam played along for his mother's sake. We made it through another day.

*****

This letter I wrote to Zellie represents the first time we felt the sting of the "year of firsts." The *year of firsts* is a term I'd either never heard of or didn't pay proper attention to. After Veronica's mother was tragically killed in a car accident, she talked about missing her mother. She'd mention special dates as they came up. I grieved horribly but didn't recognize the extra pain that Veronica was suffering.

I realize now our grief is our own. When we are close to someone, each of us will respond differently. But we begin to share a common language. First birthdays, first holidays, and the first big family-get-togethers are never the same.

For this *first*, the wound was still fresh. We lit the candles with no joy. Veronica carried the cake to Ruth, and we sang "Happy Birthday." Then Ruth and Liam blew out the candles. My eyes kept wandering toward the empty highchair that still sat near the counter next to my coffee pot. The house was indeed sad.

*****

In this stage of grief, fond memories will layer sadness upon sadness. In turn, those layers smother even the smallest pleasures in life.

Suddenly, we've all joined this sad, horrible club, which comprises good people who have lost a child or loved one. We live two lives: our normal everyday lives and the one nobody else is privy to. We can appear normal until it becomes obvious through some random outburst of grief or a small tear on the cheek. For those of us in this club, occasionally, we're able to recognize the simple meaning of someone else's blank stare.

That happened to me on a day I did not expect. I attended a breakfast meeting about a month after the funeral. Joe Sproles, a friend of mine, hurried over to me as I first walked into the room. He grabbed my hand and held on tight. He asked with such sincerity how I was holding up. "Fine," I said, not really meaning it.

He knew better and said, "Hang in there, brother."

As I sat down at a large, round banquet table, I looked over at Joe and noticed his blank stare aimed at nothing in the middle of the table. It was a familiar look. A look I remembered seeing on my son, Kevin. As I returned to the office, I asked my chief of staff, Jami Des Chenes, "Hey, Jami, how is Joe's wife feeling? I heard she wasn't well, and Joe was really quiet today."

Jami checked with friends and came back with, "Charlene is doing fine. He probably had something else on his mind."

A week later, Joe scheduled a meeting in my office on an unrelated topic. When he sat down at my conference table, I said, "Joe, I gotta be honest. I saw a look on your face the other day, and I was worried about you. Is everything okay?"

He sat quietly for a moment, and I thought I might have said the wrong thing. Then the tears flowed. He said, "I lost my little girl too. My daughter. It was about fifty years ago. It was a car accident. I was the driver."

In the previous chapter, I talked about the crashing waves of grief. Now here we sit, two men: one a month past a tragic death, the other five decades later, both reliving our own shipwrecks.

The thing that hit me the hardest was his emotion after such a long time. We're told that time will heal all wounds. Joe said, "It never goes away. There isn't a day that goes by that I don't think about her…about that day."

It really is a forever thing.

We talked a long time about our little girls. We talked a lot about what gets us through it all. Faith was our answer. He showed me an app on his phone, *Jesus Calling* by Sarah Young. I pulled out my leather-bound copy of *Jesus Calling*. I kept one at work and one at my bedside. We each read passages every day, only in different formats.

Joe Sproles worked for General Motors at the time and is almost single-handedly responsible for Michigan's seatbelt law. I'm convinced more than ever that God uses His people to act as angels for one another. The Holy Spirit put Joe and me together that week. We pray for each other, still.

*****

This summer, when I called Joe at his home to ask permission to tell his story in my book, he was quiet for a moment, and I again thought I might have offended him. Choked up, he finally said, "God bless you. You've made my morning. Yes, you can use the story."

As we said our goodbyes, he reminded me again to read Proverbs 3:5–6, "Trust in the Lord with all your heart and lean not on your own understanding; in all your ways submit to him, and he will make your paths straight."

We have no choice but to realize everything and anything in human terms. It's who we are. We lean on our own understanding of time. Oddly, at the moment of a tragedy, seconds, minutes, and hours can seem like an eternity. And then, two months or fifty years later, everything feels like it was just yesterday.

We have no concept of what eternity really means. It is truly beyond all human understanding. So we submit to the Lord. We let it go. We let Him guide our path. We have faith.

19

A Seat at the Table for God

My Dearest Zellie,

Today is Thanksgiving.

    We're staying home this year to have a quiet family dinner. Your aunt Andrea is coming to help cook and celebrate the day with us. You're Oma ordered another big turkey. It's bigger than we need to feed our small family, but you know how your Oma loves her leftovers.

    Auntie A sent over a dry brine recipe for the turkey. If you don't know what that means, it's when you rub kosher salt and brown sugar all over the turkey, then let it sit in the refrigerator until Andrea gets home to cook it.

    I took the liberty of adding a pinch of crushed red pepper to the mix because I know how much you like the hot spice. I remember how you could eat at Frank's Red-Hot right off the spoon. You are so much like your mama that way. Cayenne pepper tastes sweet on the tongue to the two of you. Hard to fathom for your Opa.

Other memories appear as I walk the dogs. I know how much you liked to wander around the block with me, with Bo and Riley leading the way. Surprisingly, they were both very patient whenever you were with us and didn't tug as hard on the leash.

Funny thing though, Zellie-belly, every time I pass the freshly painted fire hydrant on the south side of our block, I picture you climbing up and hugging it like it was your best friend. A silly memory to hold on to, I know.

You know I love being around people, but lately, I've taken to walking the dogs when it's darker out. Or when it's cold and rainy. Basically, we walk when people aren't sitting on their porches or working on their lawns. Our friends and neighbors are such caring people. It's a tough thing to convince them I'm doing okay when they catch me with clouded eyes and wet cheeks.

I realize now that grandfathers don't walk slower because they're older. They slow down to let the memory of their little girls catch up to them.

Sweetie, there isn't a moment that goes by that I don't think of you. Often, my thoughts of you end up as words on paper. Writing these letters to you act as a constant reminder that you were in my life, even if only for a painfully short while.

So today we will work our way through the preparation, toward our Thanksgiving. With that in mind (We okayed it with your papa and mama), we're setting a place for you at the Thanksgiving table.

I know I could do this directly, honey, but as long as you're right there, would you invite Jesus to join us? By my count, you make eight and Jesus will make nine. He can use your chair. Through the meal, you can sit across from Him, on your mama and papa's lap. We'll have plenty of room.

Remind Him that our home is nothing fancy and that He doesn't have to bring anything. Just Himself. We'll have lots of food. Tell Him, while it looks like we're feeding the masses, we're not serving fish. He'll get the joke. ☺

Through it all, honey, I count you as a pure blessing to be thankful for. We are also blessed with great family, friends, and neighbors. Zellie-belly, you can't believe how many people care about you. They still pray for our family every day. Your Oma and I are thankful for every one of them and wish for peace in their hearts through the holiday season.

And while I may walk slower these days, I walk with a thankful heart. I've come to believe that a thankful spirit is my window into Heaven. I'm also quite sure that through you, God lassoed my heart with a pretty pink ribbon stronger than rope. And because you've never let go, I'm being tugged along a path that leads to you. I'm thankful.

Still loving you more than the world is round — forever,
Your Opa

If it were up to me alone, I'd have been just as happy to skip Thanksgiving Day altogether. This was another one of those *firsts* for the family. A blanket of sadness lay over the top of everything we did as we planned out the day.

Pulling out and polishing the good china and silverware used to be a significant event. Getting the extra folding tables and chairs out of storage became more than just a holiday chore. This year, it required heroic effort.

Veronica and I spoke to the kids about setting an extra place for Zellie. They were agreeable, but it brought no joy to anyone as we laid her plate and silverware at the empty chair.

The thought was running through each of our heads; what in the world do we have to be thankful for? We were simply going through the motions that day; we all knew it, but nobody dared admit it. And it was the first time I really noticed the difference in how each of us dealt with our own faith.

*****

It was most obvious that Kevin was angry with God. He also felt guilty about his own inability to protect his daughter. His emotions were churning inside him so viciously that he found his own ways to numb the pain.

I realize it's an odd dichotomy to be angry with God if you don't fully believe in Him. But Kevin was left roughly asking, "If God is all-powerful, why did he let this happen to Zellie...to my family... to me?"

Sitting on the back deck late one evening, I asked Kevin if he believed in Heaven. For a long time, we sat in silence. It was dark, and I couldn't read his face. I asked a second time. It still took some time for him to answer.

Rather than a simple yes or no, Kevin began describing the process he was using to come to an answer. It's as if he were solving a math problem for his electrical engineering class. I let him work it out for a bit and took a different tack. "Let me ask it this way, where do you think Zellie is right now?"

This time, the answer was more straightforward. He shook his head slowly and said, "I don't know, Dad. I really don't."

*****

I mentioned to you I began seeking out faith-based books and movies. *The Shack* and *Heaven Is for Real* deal with anger at God. A friend gifted me with the book *Between Heaven and the Real World: My Story* written by Steven Curtis Chapman, who lost his five-year-old daughter. Each of these stories, true or fiction, asks the important questions we all ask about true faith and loss.

In hard times, we might find ourselves shaking a fist at God across a chasm we imagine being there. We shout angry words to cover the distance between us and Him, only to find out that there is no distance at all. He's right here. His peace is already in our hearts if we just look for the smallest of signs.

We each discover this knowledge in our own way. I can't tell you how often I've prayed that Kevin would get just a peek of Zellie in the lap of Jesus. But as we pray, we rarely get the answers we want; we only get the answers we need. I wish this one didn't surpass my understanding, but it truly does.

20

Remembering Zellie's Acting Debut

My Dearest Zellie,

It's Christmas Eve. Looking back over my lifetime, I've always looked forward to this day. Not so much this year, I'm afraid. Your Opa still misses you terribly.

There still isn't a moment that goes by...

Sweetie, we know that there are no tears or sorrow in Heaven, so Christmas must have a completely new meaning for you too.

While I can take comfort in knowing you're sitting on the lap of the King of kings today, short of my first goodbye to you, this one is the hardest letter I've written.

Over the past few months, I've talked to many families who have lost loved ones as well. They warned me that this is the "year of firsts." Everything we experience without you is a first.

Our friends have been so very kind. I'm convinced that you've whispered into the ears of a few strangers too. We're still receiving the kindest letters, notes, and messages, especially from those that have taken the time to share with us their own losses. They're sharing with us the things that offered them the most comfort.

I carry in my wallet a small angel medallion that was sent along with a beautiful card. I'm reading another book given to me by a friend who holds his own grandkids much tighter these days.

We have angel statuettes scattered about the house and garden, each to remind us of how precious you were. New wind chimes call out your name with every breeze. Next spring, a new rosebush will bloom for you. A gift from a friend.

They want our family to know that we're not alone. We find comfort and strength in each other. I guess that's why, in return, I share my letters to you with them.

For us, your Christmas stocking on the mantle and a tree ornament with your name on it are the most recent reminders of what a gift you were to so many of us here on earth. It's a gift that goes on when I close my eyes. In that silence, I can pick you up again and hold you close for one more morning walk. This time, the walk will be on Christmas Day, and I'll bring you to the tree to inspect all the lights, ornaments, and presents under the tree.

Do you remember last year? Liam insisted on helping open everybody's presents: his, yours, Oma, and Opa's. You were more interested in the ribbons, bows, and the growing pile of wrapping paper. Your eyes, big and brown, reminded me so much of Cindy Lou Who. The little girl from the Grinch cartoon.

Even though I've never been really Grinchy, honey, with those Christmas Day, Zellie-Lou-Who eyes, you made your Opa's heart swell seven times its size.

Today, just like Thanksgiving, you're invited to join us for the Christmas supper. Your Oma is planning a simple meal for the family. Andrea will be here to help us celebrate the day. We have pies and butter-horns from Bavarian Inn and Zehnder's. All your favorites.

Tonight, we'll go to Christmas Mass. There won't be a Midnight Mass Celebration this year. Father Bob announced both services will be earlier. He said he's getting too old to make it to midnight. Something your ol' Opa can appreciate.

Do you remember your first Christmas Mass? You were an actress in the Christmas play. Yep, you played baby Jesus. I must say that you played your part with great flair. You made quite the acting debut.

You laid on Mary's lap and announced to the congregation, in your own breathtaking way, that Jesus Christ was born! Believe me, no one in the church, even in the farthest pews, doubted that this was indeed "the day." Your Opa was so proud of you!

Zellie-belly, this year we're all going to shed tears. It's hard to imagine any Christmas in the future without you.

Santa Claus will still come for you and Liam. He'll slip some treats into your stocking by the fireplace and leave presents under the tree. We'll make it as normal as we can for your brother, despite our grown-up grief.

But, we'll also feel joy.

For us, the joy of celebration will come in a very different form. We will spend every Christmas from this day forth with a little less glitter, fewer dinner parties, and a lot less time at the shopping centers.

We will spend each year with much more reflection, wondering at the glory of the birth. We'll know that on this day, God brought into our world a flesh and blood promise that we have a path to eternal life. A promise that one day, we can all be together again. Forever.

As your Opa continues to ask God for a healing heart, I will always remember the little girl that stood in wide-eyed wonder on Christmas Day. I can never forget my little helper as you hung out with Opa to do the required assembling together.

I can't lie to you and tell you it doesn't hurt like heck. But you can still make me smile, honey. I will forever cherish the memory of my little peanut as she played Jesus in our church's Christmas Pageant and that today, you're sitting in His lap.

These days, I spend a lot of time talking to God about you. But, while you're right there, Zellie-belly, would you whisper a couple of thank you's to Him on my behalf?

First for the miracle of Jesus and this day. The other would be for you in my life. Seriously, how many men in this world, on Christmas

Day, can say they've held a true angel in their arms? Even with the ache in my heart, I feel like the luckiest grandfather ever.

Merry Christmas, sweetheart! I still love you more than the world is round — forever, Your Opa

Even though I talk about Christmas joy, I still feel as if this was one of my darkest letters because of the mood I was in at the time. The letter itself may not fully convey my emotions, but I still see traces of the deep loneliness I felt. The dark mood is easily explained because there ought to always be something special about being a grandparent at Christmas. This year, there wasn't.

Don't get me wrong. I loved being a parent at Christmas time, but there's an awful lot of pressure tied to raising your own kids. The pressure is off when you're grandpa and grandma. While parents still need to worry over baths, proper bedtimes, and diaper-changing duties, grandparents only need to wonder about how big the smiles will be on Christmas morning.

For our family, the joy of Christmas morning was more like Christmas *mourning*. Mourning fog, you could call it, I suppose. This fog blankets each and every day. December twenty-fifth feels like nothing more than one more wound that time hasn't healed yet. Waves of grief and memories, both good and bad, have no distinction during this fog. The constant sorrow fatigued us.

*****

The miracle of the Christmas story ought to be celebrated with true joy in our hearts. In the year of firsts, we simply go through the motions. We struggle to normalize life when life will never be normal again. We try to use beautiful memories to carry us through the pain of the present. Such as just a year ago, our Christmas morning was a delight because of Zellie's curious nature. She had those beautiful enormous owl eyes that sparkled as she hunted for new things to discover.

It's at these times when the oddest feelings of guilt hit—guilt for not embracing the true meaning of Christ at Christmas, guilt for the selfishness of thinking only of our own pain, guilt for feeling lonely.

Lonely? How can this even be a real thing right now? I mean, after all, the family is going through this same ordeal. We're all right here, together. But we feel so alone.

This is about the time I truly sought God's help. It was like, "Dear Lord, I know it's kind of a big day for you, with your Son's birthday and all. But I could sure use a little help down here to get me through to tomorrow!"

Veronica was going through her own set of crises as well. She was the planner. She was the faith leader. She was supposed to be the rock for Ruth, Liam, and Kevin. The household still needed to function. Dinners still needed to be made.

*****

Christmas for Veronica was already tough enough. As I mentioned earlier, three months after our Kevin was born in 1986, the day after Christmas, Veronica's mother was killed in a car crash. Marilyn Eckenswiller was fifty-two years old and died working as a rural postal carrier.

I received the call about Marilyn just shortly after arriving at our Livonia, Michigan, home, following our Christmas visit to Veronica's parents. Veronica had just laid down on the couch for a quick nap. I had to wake her with the horrible news. We packed up, put Kevin back into the car, and headed north again.

Veronica, her sisters and brothers, and her father, Leo, all experienced their own year of firsts. And yes, the first Christmas without Marilyn was the toughest. The family had to lean hard on each other. And then with Zellie, we all had to lean in again, just a little tighter.

21

Resolved to Find Peace

My Dearest Zellie,

Today is New Year's Day. A hopeful day.

I know that it's only been a week since I last wrote to you, but this letter won't be as long. I must be honest, Zellie-belly, 2017 was an awful year for us all. I'm grateful it's behind us.

Oh, 2017 started out well enough. I can't be completely mad at it. It went downhill pretty darn fast, though, I can tell you that!

I can also tell you about a couple of years I'll always treasure, 2013 and 2015. These years were both certainly gifts from God. Those are the years that Liam and you came into our lives.

Zellie-belly, the times when you and your brother were together were, without a doubt, the happiest days of your Opa's life. Oh, what I'd give to have those days back!

Honey, in church yesterday, Father Bob spoke of seeing other people with a kind of "Simeon sight." Not just looking at them, but truly seeing the person standing in front of us. Wondering about the condition of people is the best way I can put it, I guess.

It made me think that this is the kind of sight that binds parents and grandparents tightly to their kids. We consider your eyes in the first moments and days of your life, and we see your innocence, your true spirit, your potential for greatness.

When it comes right down to it, honey, I suppose we see God through the eyes of our children. We see a miracle.

It's a horrible thing losing a miracle. I guess that's why I was so mad at 2017.

Sweetheart, when you left us in September, the days stopped mattering to me. Now, days and nights are all the same. Yes, I get up in the morning and go to bed at night. But there's no joy in a sunrise. No contentment at sunset. Time just kind of plods along.

People that have suffered a sudden tragic loss will know exactly what I mean. It's like one long, cloudy day that just won't end.

So, Zellie-belly, you were indeed my personal angel. It will always amaze me how a heart can be broken and filled to the brim at the very same time.

I must say, though, while I lost my little angel, I take solace in knowing I was offered the gift of sight. And while I'm not perfect, by any means, I will continue to take my first steps in understanding the genuine miracle of God.

Happy New Year, sweetheart! Here's to holding you in my arms again one day!

I still love you more than the world is round — forever,
Your Opa

Only a week went by since my Christmas letter to Zellie, but here we are in a new year. I wrote that it was a hopeful day, and I truly meant it. I prayed over the holidays—a lot! Repeatedly, I asked Jesus to ease the pain in my heart, and again, He listened.

A friend to Veronica and me, Jerome Buckley, read my letter to Zellie and asked if I'd write a toast to 2018. Jerome is the owner and publisher of the Michigan Banner, a small minority publication that covers all things happening in the Saginaw area.

Jerome lost his wife and still grieves. When we met for coffee, we talked about how the Holy Spirit tugs at our hearts. We wondered how people with no faith can make it through their losses. This camaraderie that we share makes it easy to open up with other people. It's something I could never do in my early years.

Because I based my Michigan Banner Tribute to 2018 on my letter to Zellie, it was a simple thing to write.

Senator Ken Horn's Salute to 2018

To all my friends at the Banner,

Many of you know I lost my angel, two-year-old Zellie, in September 2017. Zellie was her Opa's little girl. She was full of life. She played and loved fearlessly. I still have a hard time thinking about her being gone. I often had to leave and come back to my desk just to finish writing about her in this salute to 2018.

At our New Year's Day Mass, Father Bob Byrne spoke of seeing people with a kind of "Simeon sight." Not just looking at them, but truly seeing the person standing in front of us. Being curious about the condition of other people is the best way I can put it.

It made me think of the kind of sight which binds parents and grandparents so tightly to their kids. We look into a child's eyes in the first moments and days of their lives. We "see" our children's innocence and spirit. When it comes right down to it, we truly see God in the eyes of our children. We see a miracle.

It's a horrible thing, losing a miracle. I guess that's why I was so mad at the year 2017.

For people who have lost loved ones, priorities can change rather quickly. I know mine have. There's not much more the world can do to a family that has lost everything. For me personally, I stopped watching TV news. I try to be more patient with impatient people.

I'm more interested in solving actual problems. I continue to be uninterested in reading political rants and gossip about people I've never met. I pray more often. I recognize that I'm not perfect, by any means.

Down deep, I strive harder to better understand the true miracles of God.

So here we are in the year 2018. A year where new perspectives and priorities can give us great hope. It'll be a busy year for all of us, for sure. But our families deserve our complete love and full attention.

Yes, there will be elections, but remember what's important inside your own home. Ranting politicians on either side aren't going to set your tables at supper time, and they won't hurry over to cut your lawn for you before you get home from work.

We'll have a new and hopefully growing economy in 2018. Maybe we'll get a chance to catch up on some old bills and do something special for our families. It will be a time of growth, hope, and happiness if we choose it to be.

Here then, comes a toast and my personal resolution for 2018:

I resolve to find peace in 2018 as I treasure the memories of my littlest angel, Zellie.

I resolve to use my newfound sight as I look at family, friends, and neighbors, to "see" them rightfully as children of God.

I further resolve to share signs of hope and joy with others as we all continue our search for peaceful hearts.

And remember, for 2018 and beyond, at the gates of Heaven, we will never be judged on the things we collect in our lifetimes. We'll never be judged by our accomplishments, no matter how great they may be. No, in the very end, we'll all be judged on one very simple thing; how we treated each other here on earth.

Happy New Year from my family to yours! We wish you joy in 2018.

— State Senator Ken Horn

22

Raspberry Tickles

My Dearest Zellie,

Today marks exactly six months' worth of Sundays since we said goodbye. While Heaven must be like, well… Heaven, down here it's kind of cold and very windy. Your wind chimes have been ringing out to us nonstop.

Your Oma was asking just today if there'll ever be a time that we can make it through Sunday Mass without misting up the way we do.

A little secret I use is to grab a sheet of paper towel and tuck it into my pocket. Honestly, a Bounty towel is much stronger than the puny tissues that your Oma keeps in her purse.

Yes, sweetheart, it has been a tough week for everyone down here. But I've experienced a few amazing signs from above. I thought you'd like to hear about one of these today.

I added some pictures of six-month-old Kasen. As his family let me hold him, he reminded me so much of you. He is quiet and curious.

When I held Kasen, he kept one hand on my shoulder as he watched my face. I could only hold him for a short while before the tears began to flow.

It wasn't long before I handed Kasen back to his grandma, Delena. We had some 400-people attending the luncheon we were at, and I didn't want them to catch me all weepy right before the award ceremony.

But Zellie-belly, I'm convinced that God sends forth His people to act as angels for each other. How else can you explain how such a faithful family as Tariq and ShaRease Price would bring their little Kasen to visit with your Oma and Opa during, of all things, an economic development lunch?

Did you know, sweetie, that Miss ShaRease used to babysit your daddy and your aunt Andrea? God created such an enormous world and then put us all together in it.

Throughout the entire meal, thoughts of Kasen brought me to thoughts of you. So I went back to Kasen and had another chance to hold him. As I blew raspberry tickles into the palm of his hand, he came very, very close to a smile.

Honey, I know God had bigger plans for you. I do hope, though, that every once in a while, Jesus blows raspberry tickles into your hand until you smile and that you'll think of your ol' Opa.

In the meantime, at this half-year mark, just remember that Opa still loves you more than the world is round. And there isn't a day that goes by…

Forever,
Your Opa

I am truly convinced that God brings His people together for one another's sake. How else could I explain how this handsome toddler ended up at a Chamber of Commerce luncheon? Meeting up with the Price family was just another sign that the Holy Spirit guides us on a common path. It truly was a joy holding Kasen.

Later that month, I met Maddy, the daughter of Chris and Jennifer Coston. Maddy was a baby when Jennifer brought her to my Lansing office for the first time. Jennifer is a volunteer advocate for the American Cancer Society, and this was their lobby day at the Capitol. Maddy was just weeks old, and mom didn't want to leave her behind, so she came to visit.

Knowing about Zellie, and at the end of our half-hour meeting, Jen asked if I wanted to hold Maddy. I sure did, and it didn't take long for the tears to show up. I can't even remember what words of comfort Jennifer had for me, but as Maddy stared up at me, I asked if it'd be okay if I could be an "Opa" to her. It's kind of funny how we blurt things out like that. But Jen smiled and said, "That'd be just fine."

I began paying attention to all kids differently, after Zellie. Even when they fuss.

I recall being at a home building center in Saginaw when a young baby started getting really loud. The baby was in a carrier in the shopping cart. Both parents seemed embarrassed by the outburst, and each was whisper-yelling at their child to be silent.

I resisted the temptation to intervene. It was none of my business after all. But I wanted to say to the parents, "Don't be mad. Let her cry, for goodness's sake. Don't you realize how precious life is, and how lucky you are?"

*****

The same week that I met Kasen at the Chamber event, the Holy Spirit put another friend to work in our lives. Kelley Keyton-Peatross, a friend to both Veronica and me, surprised us by collecting over one hundred books, all picked out and gifted by the employees of Consumers Energy where she works. Each of the books is dedicated to Zellie and bears the name of the employee friend from Consumers Energy who made the gift. They donated the books to many Saginaw County libraries.

Kelley knew of our love of the library and that Ruth, Liam, and Zellie visited nearly every day. It was one of Zellie's very favorite places to be.

Well, come to find out many people knew it too. Besides books, friends donated a plush Yertle the Turtle doll. Dr. Seuss' *Yertle the Turtle* is the book I read to elementary school kids during March Is Reading Month. I would then read it to Zellie when I came home from work.

Frankenmuth
James E. Wickson
District Library

As we delivered donated books to the Frankenmuth library, we learned of another equally touching story. Librarian Mary Chasseur informed us that when a group of friends and neighbors heard about our tragedy, they donated enough books and dollars to create some reading kits in Zellie's name.

The library creates literature kits that families can check out as they do with other books. Pam Williams put the kits together. I can tell you that Zellie loved the heck out of Miss Pam with all the visits she made to the library. This gesture was so important to our family that I'd truly like to thank the following people:

Joe and Mary Ricard
Elroy and Jean Schluckebier
Pam and Todd Williams
Frankenmuth MOPS at St. Lorenz
Mary and Tim Chasseur
Michelle and Michael Duclos

If you're ever anywhere near Frankenmuth, be sure to stop at the Wickson Library children's wing and see these books and kits. You might even see Zellie's Yertle the Turtle plush, which was featured as part of these new "Literature Kits" at the library.

*****

While I'm thinking about it, it's always a great idea to donate new and gently used books to your own local library in someone's name. You never know what family is going to be impacted by your thoughtfulness.

23

Out of the Blue

My Dearest Zellie,

Honey, this will be a brief letter. Your Oma and Opa have been experiencing some deep sadness. Especially these past few weeks. The only way for me to get this sadness out of my heart is to talk to you through our letters.

Speaking of letters, in the mail today, I received a card congratulating me on a recent accomplishment. Inside the card were two photos of you and me from the Labor Day Bridge Walk in Frankenmuth. You were so beautiful.

I remember how tired you were, but your Oma couldn't convince you to go home without your Opa. That was September 4.

Zellie-belly, had I known that within three weeks you'd be gone forever, I would have held you SO tight. I never would have let go. Jesus is patient. I'm sure He wouldn't have minded if you and I spent a little more time together.

Each day, I read from a book called Jesus Calling. It tells me that whenever I feel hurt or I'm stuck, I should just say, "Jesus, help me."

Saying it often enough is calming to me. Sometimes it works right away, and sometimes I have to say it a few dozen times in a row. I'm pretty sure that He hears me the first time, but that He gets distracted having to rescue you from the tall monkey bars in Heaven. ☺

Just know that we think about you all the time. All the time.

I still love you more than the world is round — forever,
Your Opa

This letter came out of the blue. It didn't require a holiday or any special occasion. But receiving those pictures in the mail shortly before Easter kind of triggered the need to write, I imagine.

As I mentioned previously, these letters are a release to me. They're cathartic. I suppose we all have our way of dealing with stress and anxiety, but mowing the lawn and writing are two ways for me to get the busy stuff out of my head.

Another trick I used to relieve stress is to work out at our local gym. This time, the workout wasn't working out so well. Another wave of grief crashed down on me. Believe me, I did not lose the symbolism of being on a treadmill.

Because the exercise wasn't working, I headed to the locker room. One of my favorite things about this gym was that it has both a dry sauna and a steam room. The steam is always thickest with the first visitor. When the tiles are cool, it doesn't take an enormous amount of heat to generate a dense fog.

It's the perfect place to be when you want to be alone in your grief. As the fog reaches its peak, it's impossible to see your own hand as you hold it out in front of you. In turn, no one else could see my tears should they have walked in on my anguish. This grief wave was strong. Make you rock-back-and-forth-sobbing kind of strong.

*****

As I mentioned earlier, *Jesus Calling* is a daily devotional for me. If you're not familiar with this book, author Sarah Hubbard shares scripture each day. She interprets the Bible by writing as if Jesus is actually talking to us. I know perfectly well it's the author and not Jesus talking to me, but Ms. Hubbard's words connected me closer to Jesus than I've ever been. This book played a huge role in me rediscovering and growing my faith.

The most important lesson I learned is what I wrote to Zellie, "*Each day, I read from a book called Jesus Calling. It tells me that whenever I feel hurt or I'm stuck, I should just say, 'Jesus, help me.'*"

As a fresh wave crashes down on me, this is my life jacket. I place my hand on my chest and gently pat at my heart. "Jesus, help me! Jesus, help!" If I have to repeat myself a hundred times over, that's what I'll do.

The funny thing is, though, the more I got into the habit, the easier it became. I came to find that I wasn't calling on Jesus at all. He was already here. I simply had to focus myself to center my heart. Centering is the part that became the habit.

*****

So there I sat in the sauna with arms folded around my heart, eyes closed, rocking, sobbing, repeating, "*Jesus, help me! Jesus, help me!*" Over and over, I echoed the refrain.

Out of the blue came my second vision.

With eyes closed, a dark pit appeared in the distance. I stopped rocking, focusing rather on this new thing in front of me. It was a curiosity. As you read this, if you close your eyes and imagine a deep, dark hole in the ground, you might get a foggy, blurry representation of a hole. This vision, however, was clear as day.

As I concentrated on the pit way out in the distance, I noticed that the turf was slowly folding down at the edges and breaking off into the hole. There was no sound. The pit was expanding. It didn't feel right. Not evil, just not right.

Until a dark path appeared. The path started about a step away from where I sat and led directly to the pit. I couldn't tell you what material this walking path was made of. It was simply dark. Now—this—felt evil. And it called out to me to take the first step.

I'm convinced that the Holy Spirit tugged at my back to sit perfectly still. One more time, I said, "Jesus, help me!" I never meant it more.

And then, a window opened to me. It was a perfect circle of light. And I mean perfect in every way. My curiosity returned and centered on the light as it entirely blocked the dark pit from my sight. The dark path was hidden too. I knew instinctively that it wasn't gone. The light just wasn't going to allow it to be seen.

After a quick moment, I witnessed another curious thing. Two half-circles were extending from either side of the window. It was like wings expanding, but perfectly geometric. All I could think was, *Well, that's weird!*

These thoughts washed away quickly, however, as the window of light started growing. But I realized it wasn't growing at all. It was getting closer. Not sure what else to do, I just hunkered down to wait for it to hit.

It was like a soft explosion. The light was in me. It was all around me. It was ecstasy. I found myself rocking and sobbing again but for a completely different reason. That circle of light was a window to Heaven. I met Jesus.

I never understood what it meant for Jesus to be in me and for me to be in Jesus. I didn't truly understand the whole "I am the light" thing before this. I do now.

*****

These days, a little at a time, I'm reading the Bible for the very first time. Even as I write this book, I marvel at this vision that God gifted me with. How could something like this happen to such an imperfect, unpracticed person such as me?

I saw the face of Jesus, and my life will never, ever be the same. I'm a different person than I was. As I listen to others share their stories of rebirth, my ears are now open. I know Heaven is real. Really real.

24

"I Just Had to Leave Early"

My Dearest Zellie,

The Easter Bunny came this morning. Liam spent a part of his morning searching for eggs and candies. Bocephus and Riley helped. They have pretty good basset hound noses. Bo got a bit of a head start last night and snuck a couple of marshmallow Peeps.

Just before we headed off to church, I tossed a beef brisket into the smoker because later we'll all be heading over to Aunt JoAnn's for Easter supper. Your Oma found some fresh sea bass to bake. She knows how you loved your "pescado."

The church was full today. Sweetie pie, you would have liked the music and liturgical dancers. One of the young dancers reminded me of you. There were so many kids in the pews today. It was loud and boister-ous. A beautiful thing to see.

Of course, I'm sure you were watching over us. It's your job now. I know that for sure because Liam told us you talked to him. Your mama translated Liam's words to us. You said to him, "I didn't die. I just left early to watch over everyone." He also told us "he isn't going to 'leave early' because he has great things to do, like his Oma and Opa."

I hope you keep talking to Liam. He really loves you, and he always seems in a happy mood after a visit from you.

Honey, you know that shortly after you left us early, your Oma and I witnessed a miracle together. I received a second visit from the Holy Spirit. I won't say much about it here, but I suppose you could say that I've seen the light. It's true what they say; God sure works in mysterious ways.

As much as it hurts, you've brought me closer to God than I've ever been. Whenever I need to talk to Him, I picture your beautiful face and *follow your sparkling smile all the way to Heaven. That way, when one of those waves of grief crashes over me, it's easier to ask for help and my prayers for relief are answered quick as a whistle.*

Well, Zellie-belly, considering what day it is, and with you watching over us, I can't help but think that the miracles in the Bible are real. Most importantly, the Easter story has been made real for me again. Seeds of doubt have washed away. I know that the ultimate miracle and God's gift of eternal life were given to us when Jesus died and rose again.

Easter morning can still be fun. We can enjoy coloring eggs, nibbling chocolate bunnies, and chasing the puppies away from our marshmallow peeps. All things you really enjoyed.

But Easter means much more to all of us now. Now, and until we can hold you in our arms again.

As for me, I still love you more than the world is round.

Always will. Forever.
Your Opa

Liam's sister's death truly affected him. We may never know the true scope of his trauma. Teachers and school officials kept a close eye on him for us.

Besides school officials, Veronica drove Liam to the Saginaw Children's Museum, where the entire family met with Children's Grief Center director Camille Gerace Nitschky. The partnership between the Grief Center and the Children's Museum was a true blessing. I pray that every community has a resource like Camille.

Despite the help we could locate from the outside, and the extra attention we gave him at home, Liam still had his wave-crashing moments. When you stop and think about it as hard as it is for adults to reason out their pain and feelings of loss, imagine the rocky road that kids must travel.

Even at his young age, Liam is very smart and could normally reason out typical, everyday problems as if they were just puzzles to solve. After Zellie's accident, though, we would find him shut down one minute, normal the next, and then moments later having fits of rage. He loved his sister, and this loss was one he just couldn't figure out.

He was sad. He was frightened. We were worried.

Veronica and I would pray as deeply for Liam as we did for Kevin and Ruth. The prayers seemed to help. Because one morning, Liam woke from a phenomenal dream, which he shared with his mother. What a relief it was to Veronica and me to hear Ruth translating Liam's story from Spanish.

He said that when Zellie talked to him, she said, *"I didn't die. I just left early to watch over everyone."* Then Liam added Zellie told him, *"That he isn't going to 'leave early' because he has great things to do, like his Oma and Opa."*

We could only marvel at this four-and-a-half-year-old boy coming to his mama, telling her he had a conversation with his sister in Heaven. Did Zellie really show up? Is this a construct of Liam's grief?

In either regard, this visit changed Liam. It changed him for the good. Oh, he still has his moments when a memory of Zellie catches up to him, but he's happier and more confident. He's more like himself even years later. I think that it also changed Ruth. Liam's dream comforted her. Mother and son are so close. With God's help, they give each other strength.

For me, I love the image of Zellie coming to visit her big brother in a dream. With certainty, it was a life-changing experience for Liam. Most importantly, I choose to believe that the Holy Spirit talked directly to Liam in a language the young boy could understand. How can I not believe it after all I've witnessed?

25

Help for Bocephus

My Dearest Zellie,

Lately, you've been in my thoughts day and night. I've got so many little home projects going at the same time, but I couldn't do one more chore without getting some of these words off my heart.

This wave of grief kind of started when we almost lost Bocephus. Bo is your Oma's dog. But as a puppy, he bonded instantly to you. You became the "boss" of Bo, and he loved you very much. Well, sweetie, he's been sad and mopey ever since you left early.

He was at the animal hospital in intensive care recently. The doctors were uncertain if he was going to survive. Come to find out he has Addison's disease. He can't produce enough of a certain natural steroid that helps cope with stress, and his organs are shutting down.

The doctors and nurses at the pet hospital were so good to your Bo and so kind to your Oma and me. Remember? That's the night I asked you to visit Bocephus and give him one of your famous hugs.

You know what? We thought we'd have to gurney him to the car the next morning, but even though he was weak, he walked out on his own.

We took him right to Dr. Darrow, where Bo spent another night with IVs in his leg. The doctors all said that Bo's vital signs were some of the worst they've ever seen. They aren't sure how Bo made it through. But I do. Thank you, Zellie-belly!

Honestly, though, Bocephus isn't the true reason I'm writing to you. Honey, we ALL *miss you so terribly.*

Yesterday, they invited me to a church I've never been to. The congregation was honoring all public servants. I learned they had prayed really, really hard for our family. After the service, I met so many nice people. A few of them talked to me about their own tragic losses.

I don't know why it didn't occur to me before yesterday, but the sign, the vision that your Oma and I experienced together last autumn wasn't an answer to just our prayers. It was in answer to thousands of prayers.

From that church and so many others, from people at home and around the world, even from people we've never met, the power of prayer is real.

I'm pretty sure that all those voices together were so loud that God finally just said, "Well, for Heaven's sake! Holy Spirit, go down there and show those two grandparents that this is all real and that their Zellie is in excellent hands!"

Zellie, honey, will you pass something along to Jesus for us? Tell Him, "Dang! That was a good one! Oma and Opa got the message loud and clear. And with all my heart and soul, thank you. I believe!"

Well, my little angel, I do feel better since I started this letter. Talking to you sure eases my heart. I promise I'll write again soon. I've got to get back to work now.

Remember, I'll always love you more than the world is round — forever,
Your Opa

Worry over Bocephus kicked off the need to write to Zellie, but of course, it wasn't the most important part of the letter. It's the power of prayer that I really wanted to talk about. It's part of the real mystery of faith that puzzles us here on earth.

I'm still not a complete expert in all of this, but I've seen first-hand how prayer works. And like the column of smoke that Veronica and I witnessed, we don't always get the answers we want from our prayers. We get the answers we need though.

God has a whole different sense of timing than we do. The answers come in a variety of forms and at different levels of intensity. Signs, if you will.

Just prior to writing this letter, Pastor Dominic Burkhard invited me to visit the Cornerstone Baptist Church in Swartz Creek for a day, honoring public servants. When Senior Pastor Nathan Brown invited me to say a few words, and as I looked over this congregation, it dawned on me that it wasn't my single prayers that were bringing comfort to my family. Rather, it was all the prayers going up to Heaven together, at a single time, that really caught God's attention.

And not just this church congregation, but people all over the world as well. Between our widespread family circle and all the people we've met over decades, we literally had people praying for us in all corners of the planet.

Friends from the sister-city and sister-state connections we've made in Japan were weighing in with thoughts and prayers. Local churches reached out to let us know they were praying for us. Even friends who were never overtly religious made a point of writing to tell us we were still a part of their daily prayers.

At our own church during the sign of peace, neighbors would hang on to a handshake for an extra heartbeat. After taking communion, as I sat at the end of my pew, people in the rows behind would lay a light hand on my shoulder as they passed by.

We felt less and less isolated in our loss. Being open and honest about our pain slowly dissolved those feelings of loneliness. Every card, letter, telephone call, and every sincere touch can truly make a difference.

As simple as it seems, each small gesture can act as a prayer. We are all connected. Something I talk about more in the next chapter.

26

The Stained-Glass Dream

My Dearest Zellie,

Your Oma and Opa are sharing their 35th wedding anniversary today. With a beautiful song, Father Bob Byrne blessed our marriage during today's Mass. We'll go out later today to celebrate. Throughout this day, we'll think of you as we think of you every day.

Sweetie, there's never a day and hardly a moment that goes by that your beautiful face doesn't cross our minds.

During the entire Mass today, I kept looking at the artwork within the stained-glass window, just up and to the right of the big cross.

Visitors and parishioners alike wonder at the shape it represents. To me, it looks like either a spiritual tornado or maybe a strong root that ties us all to God. It depends on my mood, I suppose.

This letter to you has been building up in me for a while now. During this time, we've observed Memorial Day. I've met with families that have lost loved ones in the line of duty. They remember every day.

When the Missing Man Table was described to us, it really hit home to me. The empty chair, the overturned cup, the single rose, all of it turned my thoughts to you.

These symbolic tributes to our lost loved ones seem to give us all something we share. It's kind of as if a spiritual tornado put our families together, all with something very awful in common.

Well, Zellie-belly, the reason I'm telling you this is because that stained-glass window came to me in a dream this week. The dream started with a swirly, radiant light. As I focused on it, it stretched out like a root, like that image in the glass.

I felt connected to Heaven. I'm certain, especially after the things that your Oma and I have seen since you left early, that a radiant light surrounds us. I imagine a cocoon of light surrounding each person on earth.

The dream showed me we are all connected to Heaven by a spiritual umbilical cord. While your pretty face has been my direct connection to God, different images of Jesus floated through the swirl of the dream. It was comforting.

That's about the time that Riley woke me up to let her out to go potty. Bocephus was grateful that I was up and about, as well.

With all of that, honey, I just miss you so much. As many words as I might put on paper, I can never describe the loneliness we feel since you left us early. I keep praying that the signs are true and that we'll see you again. All we have left is belief.

With this newly discovered faith, I have to tell you; I know exactly where I'm headed, and I'm no longer afraid of my own death. Although of course, I'm in no particular hurry for it.

And while I may show up for our reunion a little dinged and dented, I promise to always do my best to stay on the path that leads to you. I can hardly wait for the big hug that puts your little arms around my neck again.

Sweetie, I kind of went a little long with this letter. But now that I think about it, you're invited to come out with your Oma and me to our anniversary supper. We just need to finish a few chores around the house first.

I love you more than the world is round — forever,
Your Opa

There is a difference between visions and dreams. What I described in this letter was just that, a dream. A good dream though. It brought clarity to my relationship with God. I know He is out there. I know He's in me. The dream kind of put it all into perspective.

As I mentioned in my letter to Zellie, it became clear to me that we are all connected by a sort of spiritual umbilical cord. The stained-glass image in the church finally makes sense to me now. What better way to envision the nature of the Holy Spirit? It connects us directly to Jesus. We are, indeed, one with God. It's no wonder that God hears every prayer because there is this very direct connection.

Trust me, I recognize that this is simply my personal image of how things are. This is still so far beyond my understanding. But I feel like we each need to find a way to wrap our human brains around this relationship with the Lord.

What I really like about the spiritual umbilical cord image is that when our souls are all connected to God in this way, then we are all connected to each other. When we need it the most, the Holy Spirit can draw us together in ways we don't yet fathom.

Plus being connected so directly makes the power of prayer make sense too. I think back to the thousands of people who prayed for our family as they learned of our loss. I heard someone describe their own faith in prayer, saying, "Let me know what you need. By golly, I can pray the warts off a toad if I need to."

*****

We always hear that even a whisper of a single prayer is always heard. I can only imagine the collective energy of community prayer. It is so extraordinary. Equally important as prayer is recognizing the signs that God is giving us through this connection.

I'm convinced that we all feel the signs, but we aren't always open to them. It can be as simple as thinking that something just doesn't feel right. Maybe it's churning in your belly, saying, "Don't do that" or "Don't go there!" Perhaps you feel a small push on your back that says, "Over there, see that person? Go! Help them!"

Of course, we never know what we don't know. We probably miss most of the signs sent our way. It's likely that we only see the most urgent signals as the Holy Spirit adds a firm nudge or two.

I've said many times that I'm convinced that God sends forth his people to act as angels for each other. People have shown up for me at the oddest times. Sometimes when I didn't even know I needed them. As I look back on my life with a new set of eyes, however, I appreciate other people more and more.

Today, as I remember an unsolicited act of kindness or a gentle piece of advice from the past, I look straight up to Heaven. "Thank you, Jesus!" No other words seem necessary.

27

Holding You, I've Held Everything

My Dearest Zellie,

Today would have been your third birthday. I mentioned in my last letter how tough this month of September would be for your whole family. But here we are.

Your papa is still hurting so much. We had a long talk about you last night. I think normally we would talk about what gifts to give you on your birthday. Instead, we spoke about what a gift you were to us.

Your mama and Liam are still in Ecuador. I can only imagine that your mama is thinking about you every moment of every day. This day, three years ago, was one of the most precious days in her life. You were God's gift to her.

Liam thinks about you, but I understand that you still talk to him a lot. That's good. I know he loves you. He and mama will come home to us soon. School has started, and Liam will have lots of stories to tell his teachers and classmates. Stories about mountains and waterfalls, picking fresh fruit, and befriending a "lowland paca."

Honey, I have to tell you about this video we created for you. Earlier this week, your Oma and I were sitting on the back deck and heard a song from a man called Garth Brooks called "The Dance." She asked me how we could make a picture collage of you with a song in the background.

I'm not blessed with a talent for mixing music and pictures, but I'm blessed with friends who are. We went to work right away to blend the perfect tribute to your birthday.

Yes, Zellie-belly, this is such a bittersweet day for all of us. Like the song, we just can't avoid the pain because we wouldn't have missed a minute of dancing with you here on earth. You are our sunshine!

I hope the angels bake you a special cake and that Jesus remembered to place three candles on the top. We'll all be holding you even tighter to our hearts today.

Happy birthday, sweetheart. Remember that we love you more than the world in round — forever,
Your Opa

Zellie would have been three. We were almost past our year of firsts. Each of us, still weakened by loss, had grown stronger in different ways. There were still times when I'd be triggered by the smallest things like a song on the radio, photos on the fridge, or certain sounds and smells.

In the process of learning to cope, I found myself at a small funeral reception for a family friend in the basement of St. Lorenz Lutheran Church. The officiating pastor took hold of my elbow as he shook my hand. He didn't let go and asked, "How are you doing?" For him, this question wasn't a throwaway opening line.

When I tossed him the old, "I'm doing fine" line, he locked his eyes on mine and asked again, "How are you really doing?" In that moment, I realized I was looking past him, trying to find a corner to sit and be alone, again. It's a bad habit I had gotten into over the course of my grief.

This time, as I answered the pastor, I focused back on him as a person and said, "I'm doing better. Every day is a little better."

He gave me a gentle smile this time. "Now, that's an honest answer. Thank you. We're still praying for you and your family."

*****

As I wrote this *Holding You* letter, Ruth and Liam were in Ecuador, visiting Ruth's family. Kevin flew with them, settled them in, and flew back home again for work and school. Since we failed in our attempt to get her mother Marci, sisters Glida and Meli, and niece Karen to America, Ruth desperately needed this visit. Ruth also needed the holistic medicinal powers of her father Ricardo Chongo, a Shaman healer, an important central figure in and around his village.

Secretly, Veronica and I worried that Ruth would decide not to return. She promised she loved living with us and that she and Liam would come back. But there have been so many twists and turns in this immigration story, we couldn't help but worry. I couldn't imagine losing Liam to another country. Or Ruth, for that matter. We've grown to love her. It's as if she's always been with us.

As the worry played itself out, what would Kevin do if Ruth decided it best to stay in Ecuador? I'm certain that he'd give up everything here to be with his wife and son. Veronica and I prayed over this one. We talked it through. We had no control over the decisions that Ruth and Kevin might have to make.

While all these thoughts were playing themselves out in our heads, life went on in Frankenmuth. We think of Zellie every single day. Not a moment has gone by without a memory floating through it.

*****

Missing our family, Veronica and I sat on the back deck with our iPads, going through our photos and videos of Zellie. In one video, Oma had just taught Zellie how to dance to some Scottish folksong. Zellie was spinning and clapping with the music. Her happiness recalled our little spins in the morning just before breakfast. Life is surely a dance.

It's ironic that Garth Brooks' "The Dance" was playing in the background. I have no clue what motivated Garth Brooks to write this song. I always thought it was about a girlfriend leaving or a divorce, never considering it a funeral song until that evening. It perfectly describes true loss, however.

One of my early letters to Heaven said, "*When I think about the grief we feel down here, it seems that the tighter we hang on to each other, heart and soul, the harder it is to let go. A sudden death like yours is literally a blunt-force trauma to each of us that are left behind. The pain is very real. And if given the choice between this real, physical agony and forgetting your beautiful face, I choose you. The pain I can live with.*"

The more I thought of life as a dance and thought about all the little dances with Zellie, the more these lyrics took on a whole new meaning. I would not give up a moment of the love we shared.

As we put together a collage of Zellie's photos and videos, the lyrics and music fit together beautifully. Nobody else had to see our photos with this music paired up. It was something that only the two of us needed.

"The Dance"

Garth Brooks

Looking back on the memory of
The dance we shared 'neath the stars above
For a moment all the world was right
How could I have known that you'd ever say goodbye

And now I'm glad I didn't know
The way it all would end the way it all would go
Our lives are better left to chance

I could have missed the pain
But I'd have had to miss the dance

Holding you I held everything
For a moment wasn't I a king
But if I'd only known how the king would fall
Hey who's to say you know I might have changed it all

And now I'm glad I didn't know
The way it all would end the way it all would go
Our lives are better left to chance
I could have missed the pain
But I'd have had to miss the dance

Yes my life is better left to chance
I could have missed the pain
But I'd have had to miss the dance

28

Ending the Year of Firsts

My Dearest Zellie,

Today marks the day on my calendar that you left us early. This is a somber day. Memories are flooding in like crazy.

My sweet Zellie, while I'm surrounded by people I dearly love, you bonded yourself so deeply into my heart that part of it ripped away at your leaving. I think we all feel this way.

There are no tears in Heaven, no sadness. So forgive me for this expression of pain that I write about to you. I'm pretty sure that God just wants me to get this out of my system now.

I could use your help again. Keep reminding me to use the words thank you more often as I think of you in Heaven. And especially since God is right there with you, could you ask Him a question for me? What is it He'd like us all to have learned from the past year?

I imagine that in His best George Burns voice from the movie Oh, God! He'll remind us that Heaven is real, that there is only a thin veil between there and here, and that we are all His children.

He'd go on to say that we are all filled and surrounded by a holy light and that's how He sees us. He'll tell us we are all connected to Heaven together and that we are all connected directly to each other. God charges us with the duty of knowing at least this much, and He charges us with the duty to care for and nurture each other…to be kind to everyone.

Well, that's what I figure He'd say, anyway.

In the meantime, Zellie-belly, our year of "firsts" is finally at an end. Our first Thanksgiving away from each other: the first Christmas, New Year, Easter, your birthday. Now the first anniversary of you leaving "early to watch over us."

I know this letter is long, sugar pie, and you probably want to go play with your new friends. Just remember how much we love you. And miss you.

And remember, "You are my sunshine, my only sunshine. You make me happy when skies are gray. You'll never know dear how much I love you. Please don't take your sunshine away."

I love you more than the world is round — forever,
Your Opa

So the year of firsts comes to an official end. This letter marked a year to the day that I lost my Zellie. I can't help but look back and count my blessings. It was a year of true spiritual growth.

I prayed over this newest letter to Heaven more than any other to Zellie. The previous letters came out of nowhere and were direct from the heart. They relieved pain. This letter was more of a short reflection on my journey into faith.

When I prayed over this letter, it was mostly an appeal to God, asking what He expects of me. It's like,

"Jesus, you showed me all this cool stuff. What do you want me to do with it?

"What's the bottom line here, God?

"Was all this to heal my heart and to put me on a path to you? Do you want me to witness for you?

"Are you preparing me for some unseen battle that you want me to fight at your side?"

There are millions of people with broken hearts and souls in the world. I'm just one of them. Maybe those millions of people have had their own experience with visions directly from Heaven, but so far, I've not met many yet.

As I contemplate, I can only be grateful. I went from crisis to Christ. My grief journey transformed into a faith journey. In return for the gifts that were given to me, the most important question I can ask is, "Lord, what is it I can do for you?"

This inspired this second-to-the-last letter to Zellie as I wrote, *"I will read this letter over a hundred times over before I send it, wondering if it's the right message God wants me to share with the world."*

I did indeed read over that letter a hundred times. And vacillated a hundred times more before I hit the send button. With every hesitation, I asked for wisdom. It's exactly the process I went through in deciding to write this book.

Am I doing this for me, or am I doing this for the Lord? Am I approaching my role as a witness with hubris or humility?

Over the course of the year, as I wrote my letters to Zellie, I did not consult with anyone, including Veronica. She read them for the first time as I published them on my personal social media page. I received many comments and messages from friends who were comforted by the honesty. They were telling me they did not feel so alone after reading the letters.

So I approached our family story with great humility. And it worked out that each time I really needed to get something off my chest, I'd simply write. Then friends would write back, expressing gratitude. We helped each other.

Some encouraged me to share my collection of letters. Through this whole process, and when I accepted the fact that I was so imperfect, I just handed it all up to God. Overall, it kind of felt like a win/win situation.

*****

From the days of my summer of content, and through the worst of my grief, I recognize the transformation that true faith has brought in me. Over the course of the year, people who I work with in my office remarked about my change; how differently I handled people and issues.

At work and at home, I was truly discovering, for the first time, what faith-based living was all about. These changes manifested themselves in a variety of ways, sometimes rather subtle, other times more obvious. In the subtle ways, my ears feel as if they're tuned into a different frequency: *"eyes that see and ears that hear."*

In my position, listening is always an important part of problem-solving that must constantly happen. Tuning in more closely to what others say draws out their sincere intentions.

If I find my mind wandering at any point, I literally ask the Holy Spirit to bring me back to the person in front of me. When the engagement is genuine, solutions seem to spring up out of nowhere. My job seemed to get easier and more rewarding with this new attitude.

In a different but more obvious way, I literally stamped my principles of faith into steel. Over time, I've received a number of "challenge coins." Challenge coins are kind of like business cards but without addresses and phone numbers.

Instead, the coin can describe your vocation or who you are as a person. There's a permanency to a coin that lays out your goals, objectives, or principles.

Once I considered designing my own challenge coin, it wasn't all that hard to lay out both sides of it. The front is the silhouette of the Michigan Capitol dome with my name and title. On the back is my family crest with three important words to describe my service: *faith*, *family*, and *community*.

After losing Zellie, these three words took on a much bigger meaning for me. Faith, family, and community are so much more intricately intertwined than I had ever imagined.

*****

In my homelife, I've become much bolder in sharing my rediscovered faith. I'm no longer shy about expressing my belief in the Holy Trinity. For instance, on my faith journey, I came across the movie, *An Interview with God*, and one of the more intriguing questions was, "If God were to grant you one miracle today, what would you ask for?"

I shared this question with a group of friends, but it is actually a trick question. There really isn't a final, genuine question, or answer, for any person. It is the exercise of thinking about God that is important, not what you ask of God. Because as I discovered, God doesn't give me what I want; He provides what I need.

For me, I've already received my miracle. These days, the only thing that scares me is losing what I found in my new connection with God. I know for certain that I'm the only one who can bust up this relationship. So I'm much more afraid of myself than I am of God.

Because this all falls solely on me to simply not walk away, I have to pay attention and pray when I'm fearful. If I ever struggle to think of just the right words to pray, it dawns on my heart to set aside all my foggy thoughts and say simply and clearly, "Help me, Jesus!"

Funny how it works every time.

29

Little Sister on the Way

My Dearest Zellie,

It's been so long since I've written to you. It's Mother's Day, and we celebrate both your Oma and your mama. I have some news I can't wait to share with you. Your mama will be a mother again.

Yes, Zellie, honey, you're going to have a little sister! A baby girl is on the way!

Isn't that exciting? She'll arrive in July, a week or two after my birthday. Well, you knew this all along, didn't you? You closely watch over us, and I'm sure you've had this conversation with your mama early on.

I guess I waited so long because I wanted to be certain, for myself, this was really happening. I prayed very hard that your mama and the baby would both be healthy. We all prayed.

When your mama and papa came home from a recent doctor's visit with the ultrasound pictures, we knew. Your sister is happy, healthy, and getting ready for the world.

It's funny to think with the way she's growing and kicking, will the world be ready for her? I told your papa that the perfect name for your sister might be Joy. With a gentle smile, he shook his head, and then he put me to work. I'm pretty sure it was just to keep me busy, but Kevin assigned me the task of narrowing down a list of name choices.

It might sound a little geeky, but I bought a book of popular baby names and created an actual spreadsheet. (You remember what a spreadsheet is, right? You sometimes used to sit on my lap at the desk while I was working.) Anyway, I started with a thousand baby girl names. I worked the list down to two hundred, and then to forty great names. I had your Oma do the same thing.

Sweetie, I have no clue what your sister's name will end up being. Heck, in my heart, I think your mama already has a name picked out. Either way, it was a fun exercise.

Yes, today is Mother's Day. And while I can't imagine anybody missing you more than I do, I know that can't be true. Your mama would give anything in the world just to hold you one more time. Even when she smiles, there's still a nagging sadness in her eyes.

Your mama Ruth is such a kind soul. She is so gentle and loving with Liam. She was with you too. Do me a big favor, sweetie pie, keep hugging your mama's heart. Let her know that you'll help her raise your little sister…that everything's going to be okay.

On this Mother's Day, I think it's important to remember that God walked with each of us, hand in hand, as we lived through the pain and hurt of losing you. He brought us safely through a very dark valley.

He is still walking with us, hand in hand, as he sets us on a new, more joyful path. We'll enjoy this journey together, here on earth, until we meet again.

Zellie-belly, you will always be with us, every day. I promise I will love your sister as I loved you. My new job will be to teach her that Heaven is real. Really real. And that she has a big sister. A beautiful, wonderful angel sister that will always watch over her.

Honey, I love you more than the world is round. Forever.

Your Opa

So, here we are at the final letter to Heaven. I still think of my little girl every single day though there was a long gap in my writing. The delay came with good reason though. This letter announces Zellie's new sister.

While I could finally make this announcement that I'm going to be a grandfather again, our family had to be darn certain this was going to happen.

Our family learned the hard way to be very cautious when speaking about the possibility of a new child. When Ruth told us she took a pregnancy test and tested positive, our hearts leaped for joy. Within weeks, however, there was a miscarriage. The physical pain and newfound grief that Ruth dealt with were unbearable to watch.

A few months later, Ruth was pregnant again. There were no high fives. No celebrations. There was just a silent, hopeful mood that blanketed the household. It seemed to take, and then it didn't. Ruth lost this one as well.

Among other reasons, these losses were why Ruth desperately needed time. She had to recenter herself physically, mentally, and spiritually. Ruth needed to be fully prepared, with grief resolved as much as possible, and ready to open a new chapter in her life.

This was one more reason she went home to visit with her mother and family in Ecuador. Both she and Liam needed the love of mama Marci and the healing power of papa Ricardo.

When the time came, Ruth and Liam were ready to return home. In my heart, I still believe that Ruth might have stayed in Ecuador. But she realized that Liam's best chances for an excellent education and a bright future were here in the United States. Veronica and I felt great relief the moment we spotted the two of them coming off the plane at Detroit Metro.

It wasn't too long after returning to us that Ruth and Kevin announced Ruth was pregnant again. We could only hope that Ruth's therapeutic trip would make all the difference this time around.

Ruth seemed to be doing well for a period of time, and hopes were high. Until she started feeling pain again. And the bleeding started. Kevin took her to the emergency room. And...we prayed.

I prayed to the Holy Spirit for hours. I prayed myself into tears. I had never, ever meant it this much. I already knew the power of prayer, but I pushed this one to the limit.

"Holy Spirit, you revealed yourself to me. I know You're there. Jesus, I'm yours. I belong to You. I need You now. We can't lose this baby. I'm asking You to heal Ruth, to stop the bleeding. Please…for Ruth, for the baby, for our family!"

Over and over and over! And it worked! The bleeding stopped, and Ruth grew stronger. The rest of the pregnancy went smoothly, with lots of support and countless doctor visits. This chapter's letter came shortly after a beautiful ultrasound photo of the baby.

On July 12, two days after my birthday, Aaliyah Kerrigan Grefa-Horn was born at Covenant Hospital in Saginaw, Michigan. She is gorgeous. Kevin and Ruth took bets on how fast it would take me to come up with a nickname. Of course, it didn't take long. I called her Allie on our first visit.

Allie is her own little girl, but I am truly convinced that she gets a little coaching from her big sister. She is a real spitfire. Not quite as fearless as Zellie, but every bit as curious.

The last time I met for an editing session with my friend Stefanie, I realized something especially important that had completely slipped my mind. In all the writing that I've done and all the letters that I've written to both Zellie and Liam, I've never penned out a letter to Allie K.

As I finish this book, I will remedy this oversight.

30

Love Big

Dear Allie K.,

Today is your birthday. You're turning two. Your Oma and Opa are traveling today and wish we could give you the world's biggest hugs. Expect them when we get home to you.

In the meantime, your mama sent us some photos of you in your new birthday dress. Well, you are as pretty as Opa has ever seen you.

And it reminded me of one very important thing; until today, I've never written you a letter.

That might not seem too odd for you right now, sweetie, 'cause how would you know? But I have to admit that I'm running late. When your big brother and sister were born, I wrote letters to them regularly.

I wrote to say hello, and then I wrote to pass along Opa's tips for growing up. I have some catching up to do; it seems.

The photo of you looking up to Heaven is so perfect, and it really struck me to my heart. I need to tell you why.

I've been working on a project at my desk that caused me to reread my letters to your big sister, Zellie.

I read those letters over and over again. It was one of the hardest things I've ever had to do. In one of my letters to Zellie, I promised her I'd teach you all about her big sister, who had to leave us early.

And that right there is what caused the delay in my first letter to you. Where do I begin? How…do I begin?

Honey pie, as you grow older, you are becoming such a beautiful girl. You are funny, determined, and I'd even say industrious with the way you like to move rocks and dirt around the backyard with Opa.

And you are different from your sister. This is the way it should be. But this is the hard part for your old Opa. I was so afraid of losing the memories of Zellie that I looked for hints of her in our newest little girl.

It didn't take me long to realize that I didn't need to do that. You are you, and Opa loves you so, so much. You are a miracle to us!

You make me wonder how God could send another little girl to our family that we could love with ALL our heart. But then again, He's God! Miracles are kind of routine for Him, I'm thinking.

So, Allie-berry, I won't make the same mistake twice. Plus I will keep my promise to Zellie. And I will teach you everything on earth that a grandpa needs to teach little girls about growing up.

Just be prepared for the fact that this might cause your mama to have to change your clothes three or four times a day.

Happy birthday, Allie! You made me remember God gives us the power to love big. He gives us the room in our hearts for more than we can ever imagine.

Your Oma and I love you more than the world is round.

Forever,
Your Opa

Here we are in the Summer of 2021, and I found the courage and inspiration to write my first letter to Aaliyah. Veronica and I were in South Dakota for my last year in the leadership rotation for the Midwest Legislative Conference. We celebrated my July tenth birthday in Rapid City with a few colleagues who flew in early for the conference.

Allie's birthday is two days later than mine. Kevin and Ruth texted us a couple of photos of Allie in her new dress and shoes. The picture of her looking up to the sky and a few prayers in the same direction were the inspiration for this new letter.

Writing it wasn't different from every letter I sent to Zellie; the words just seem to show up. Lying in the hotel bed with the sun rising, my thoughts began coming together. I got up out of bed, splashed a little water on my face, and microwaved yesterday's coffee as I prepared to sit down at the keyboard.

As with my previous letters, it didn't take over fifteen to twenty minutes to finish. It's the self-editing and the self-doubt that take so much time. I reread the letter dozens of times. Each time, I'd find a missing word or a jumble of words to sort back out again.

And there were tears!

*****

All these years, I dreaded the thought of having to let go of Zellie. I did not want to *move on* and put her behind me. Of course, the reality of Zellie hit me a long time ago, but I swore I'd never let her vanish from my life. And I won't. I don't have to.

With Aaliyah, I never wanted to think of her simply as a rainbow baby. Meaning that she isn't a replacement for Zellie. Indeed, Allie is definitely her own person. She has a character both different and maybe a bit like Zellie. There's no reason Allie can't be Opa's little girl too.

Why did I wait so long to tell the story of Zelda? More importantly, why did I wait so long to admit that I loved Aaliyah with all my heart? Pain, grief, guilt. These are three good reasons for anyone of us when we're emotionally hanging on for dear life.

The risk of loving and losing is always a very real possibility. The risk of loving big and losing a second time can be frightening.

But a funny thing happened; about ten minutes into writing my letter to Allie, and without pausing at the keyboard, it hit me that God had given me another gift. He opened my eyes to see that our hearts are big enough to love without end. The guilt was gone.

Aaliyah is healing hearts. Kevin is like a new man when he's around her. His kindness and patience with her, even during two-year-old tantrums, remind me of myself as a young father. Even with all the pain and guilt that he felt, his love for all three children is overpowering the pain. God is love, and I see it in my son.

Ruth smiles and laughs more often with both children. Liam is the best big brother ever as he plays with and dotes over Allie. Veronica smiles more now too. And the house is not so sad anymore.

I realized that as we placed our hearts and souls in God's hands, He returned the favor. He let us know we are not alone and that we never lose our loved ones forever because *Heaven is real.*

These three words aren't just words of comfort.

We will all continue to love and cherish the memories of our little Zellie. And Opa will not hesitate to love Allie as big as the world is round—forever.

31

Wrapping It Up

Four years ago, the world crashed down on my shoulders so hard that it drove me to my knees. I had choices to make: look up or look away. I could have avoided a lot of pain by looking away and divorcing myself from the reality that Zellie was gone.

I chose to look up. I didn't invent the line "From crisis to Christ"; it just fit. As I look over my entire life, I still see the many times that the Holy Spirit nudged me along and kept me on a certain path that led to today.

Again, I ask myself, *Why did it take four years to complete this book?* With the letters to Zellie already written, heck, I was halfway there. But I needed what most people need—closure and inspiration. I received some closure when Aaliyah Kerrigan was born. The inspiration then came from the fear that I was losing Zellie all over again.

I couldn't see her face in my mind. Her voice was fading. As I said in my letters, if it's a choice between forgetting her beautiful face or living with the pain, I choose Zellie. The pain I can live with.

Pushing through the heartaches, I began pouring over her photos again. Before I knew it, letter by letter, the book began writing itself.

*****

It's funny how thoughts just pop into your head when you're this focused. As I get to this late chapter, another question occurred to me: If my spirit is continuing along this path, and if I'm connected to Heaven by a spiritual umbilical cord, am I literally in a spiritual womb? We are in our mother's womb for about nine months. Is it like that for us as we live out our lives here on earth?

I think about Jesus up on the cross and wonder at the words, "It is finished!" And in a span of a thunderclap, it's done. We have nothing left to "do" except to have faith that God has us wrapped in the loving womb of Heaven. Questioning no one else's belief or faith, being *reborn* suddenly makes all the sense in the world to me.

*****

In the meantime, here we are on earth. Following a tragedy such as ours, people will try to remind us that time heals all wounds. Indeed, after generations of footsteps, even granite stair steps will show signs of wear. In our short lives, memories will go on and on. The pain will continue to exist. It's just not as sharp. The corners are rounded by time.

The stress of loss affects everyone differently. Some look up. Some look away. The choice made here can alter the course of daily life. Some will embrace God; some will divorce Him in anger, and everything in between.

When I accepted Jesus, I embraced my family more tightly. I've witnessed the opposite in some families. As a grieving person pushes God away, they can push each other away as well.

I made the conscious decision to visualize the image of Jesus with my Zellie sitting in His lap. That's about the time that people of faith started showing up in my life. Or…about the time I noticed them in my life.

Four years ago, the day after Zellie's accident, the first door I opened found Jami Des Chenes standing on our front porch with two sacks of groceries. She didn't want us to have to worry about planning dinner.

God sends good people into our lives. Like Stephanie Rachel, who began following my letters to Zellie. Stephanie would unexpectedly Facebook message at some of my darkest moments. These personal contacts were incredibly timed, with only one explanation: The Holy Spirit guided them. Jami and Stephanie would become among the biggest cheerleaders for this book.

Truth be told, the best people God sends to us, He may have sent to us some forty years ahead of our greatest need. Veronica was always the first to encourage me to follow my dreams and passions. She backed me when I decided to buy the business, when I chose to run for elected office, and when I decided it was time to complete this book.

*****

And, of course, there are other friends and strangers, who will simply show up for you. There is always help and comfort for anyone looking for it. Sometimes it comes at us a little sideways. I never met Sarah Young. But a friend gifted her book *Jesus Calling* to me, and Ms. Young's writings set me on a righteous path.

*****

Just today, as I wrap up my book, I received a text from Pastor J. D. Howell. It read, "Just wanted to let you know that I was thinking about you and praying for you today."

I wrote back, "Thank you!!! Today was Zellie's birthday."

His response was, "Wow. I did not realize, but it was no accident that the Lord put you on my heart today."

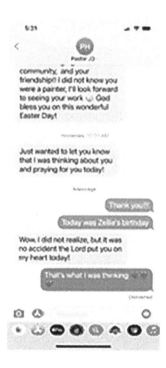

After this exchange, the Lord put it on my heart to visit a friend who had just lost her granddaughter in a drowning accident. When she opened the door, she said, "You shouldn't have to come by. I'm in a really dark place right now." When I didn't turn around to leave, she pointed at two empty rockers. We talked for half an hour on her front porch.

"Will this pain ever end?" she asked.

"No. I'm afraid not. Sounds strange today, but you don't want it too. One day, at your own pace, you'll be able to cope with it."

She talked about her granddaughter, and the memory coaxed a small smile out of her as we sat in those chairs. I remember how hard it was to talk about Zellie at first. I also recall that it then brought me comfort to say her name out loud.

*****

Earlier this same day, on the lawn of the Michigan Capitol building, the House of Representatives held a ceremony for the twentieth anniversary of the 9-11 tragedy. I walked outside in time to hear a friend, former Army Sergeant Douglas Szczepanski, do the invocation. He came up to my Capitol office afterward, and he prayed for me. It was a prayer for Zellie and me, actually.

Doug was severely injured in the line of duty. Scarred and blind in one eye, he earned the right to live life bitterly if he chooses to, yet he doesn't. And he doesn't hesitate to tell you how blessed he is. Jesus was in his life and guided him through the toughest of times. If your group or church ever needs a little spiritual booster shot, Doug Szczepanski has a gift.

Indeed, the Lord was directing traffic all day that day for me. He sent his people to me as I needed them in the morning and guided me where I needed to be in the afternoon.

*****

I started this book by admitting how imperfect I was in my faith. While I'm still as imperfect as everyone else on earth, my faith today is unshakeable.

I'm reading the Bible for the very first time. In truth, I'm listening to the Bible being read. I'm part of Brian Hardin's worldwide "global campfire" through the *Daily Audio Bible*. Each day, he reads a passage from the Old Testament, the New Testament, from Psalms, and from Proverbs. We're well over halfway through the Word as I write this in October.

After what our family has been through with our loss of Zellie and after the visions which Veronica and I experienced, it all makes sense now. I described the two windows to Heaven that opened for me. With these powerful visions as my anchors, I learn the Bible is indeed the most extraordinary book written.

The *pillar of clouds*, first mentioned in the *Book of Exodus*, hit me like a ton of bricks as I recalled the column of smoke that Veronica and I saw. The dark pit and the subsequent light that came over me in my darkest moment are both affirmed in scripture.

The spiritual umbilical cord I talk about came to me as a dream, not a vision. I recognize that my use of the term *umbilical cord* is simply a construct of my imagination. However, it brings clarity to the readings regarding us as being one body in Christ. The Lord is in us, and we are in Him. I get in now.

*****

It is highly likely that each of us has our own story of loss to tell through the death of a loved one, through a divorce, or through some catastrophe we've faced. We will cope with it in our own ways, and we will feel alone. But we aren't.

As if to prove this point, the Holy Spirit sent one more angel my way. It was toward the end of this summer and nearing the completion of this book; I met Orthodox Rabbi Elimelech Goldberg in my office in Lansing.

Rabbi G., as the children call him, created an organization over twenty years ago using martial arts as a therapy for sick children, called Kids Kicking Cancer. Kids Kicking Cancer is a unique program that teaches kids the important, confidence-building tenets of martial art. In addition, he has now created the *Heroes Circle*, inspired and taught by children with cancer for *all* kids to learn how to self-regulate and take control of their young lives.

Having a black belt myself, I connected instantly with Rabbi G. What sealed our friendship, however, was discovering that we both belonged to that "exclusive, awful-to-be-part-of club," which I mentioned earlier in this story.

Rabbi began Kids Kicking Cancer after losing his first child, Sara Basya, to leukemia at age two. He shared his book with me, *A Perfect God Created an Imperfect World Perfectly.*

In turn, I shared with him the manuscript for *Letters to Heaven.* I asked him to be honest and to review it with a critical eye. A few days later, on the anniversary of Zellie's passing, I found this in my email inbox.

*****

Dear Ken,

I pray that I am not intruding on this special day. In our tradition, the soul of the departed returns even closer on the anniversary of their passing. I pray you feel Zellie's closeness.

In life, beginnings are often celebrated, and endings are a common cause of sadness. On my journey, however, I have come to different conclusions. I now know that even the darkest night can produce the most of beautiful of sunrises.

Your Zellie and my Sara are still teaching the world!

I truly hope that I am not overstepping boundaries, but after reading your letters to Heaven, it came upon my heart to pen a very special letter from Heaven. My heart told me Zellie would want to respond to her Opa.

Again, I hope I haven't gone too far. I just wanted you to see this.

Warmly,
Elimelech

*****

I immediately opened the attached letter. After reading it, I handed it to Veronica. With tears in her eyes, which mirrored mine, she said, "You have to add this to the end of your book. So I did.

And as this story comes to an end, our hope doesn't have to. In peace, we collectively wait for a new chapter of happiness and health in our lives. And we pray for joy in our hearts as big as the world is round.

As we conclude this book, I am privileged to share with you this letter *from* Heaven.

*****

Dear Opa,

Thank you for all of your letters to Heaven. I did not need to read them to know the pain you feel at my leaving you early. And, yes, in Heaven, I can read just fine.

I can see the depth of despair in your eyes too, even when they aren't clouded with tears. I feel your heart when your eyes are closed. Beyond the grief and all the questions, your love letters have granted me another layer of purpose to the days of my life there on the earth.

For within your words and your newfound prayers, you have discovered a truth that not everyone has learned. In writing about my journey to this magnificent place called Heaven, you have grown to recognize that we are not far apart.

In your study of Genesis, you learn that at the beginning of Creation, Heaven and earth were one. Light and darkness existed together, and it was a perfect place of a magnificent Garden in Eden.

Opa, what you and I have accomplished together is opening new doors for people. It's bringing Heaven back down to earth. This expression of faith is a very important mission.

You have infused light even into the darkest of places. We can share this insight with others who know pain. You have given meaning to my two years beyond what most people might accomplish in a century.

In Heaven, there is no time. On earth, yes, the loss of a child is so very tragic. However, in Heaven, the greatest tragedy is to see a person who is ninety-five years old, dying, and doesn't have a clue as to why he lived.

That is a genuine reason to cry.

Opa, I love you, but I don't miss you because I see you all the time. Thank you for your "letters" because they tell me you can see me too. You see me in your prayers. You see me in the joy of my brother and sister. There is a growing awareness of Heaven for all the people who you share our story with.

We will be together again. But don't rush to get here. There are so many things that yet to accomplish on earth, which decorate the halls of Heaven. Spread your "letters." Tell people they don't even need a stamp as they decide to write too.

All they need is a prayer and a little light to see the bridge that truly unites our Heaven above with the earth below.

Opa, you and I will continue to light the road for others…until the day we are walking on it together.

With love as big as both Heaven and earth,
Your Zellie-belly

Remember, there are many forms of loss that we all face in a lifetime. But you should never feel alone. Occasionally, the help you get will come from the most unexpected places.

From the smallest gesture of faith to really big things; like letters *from* Heaven, God will send you exactly the people you need when you need them the most.

Have faith.

Because Heaven is real. Really real.

Grateful for These Sources

Sarah Young (2004). *Jesus Calling: Enjoying Peace in His Presence*. Nashville, TN: Thomas Nelson, HarperCollins.

William P. Young (2007). *The Shack: Where Tragedy Confronts Eternity*: Windblown Media, FaithWords, Hodder & Stoughton.

Todd Burpo and Lynn Vincent (2010). *Heaven Is for Real: A Little Boy's Astounding Story of His Trip to Heaven and Back*: Thomas Nelson, HarperCollins.

Steven Curtis Chapman and Ken Abraham (2017). *Between Heaven and the Real World: My Story:* Rebell, Baker Publishing Group.

An Interview with God (2018). Movie.

Garth Brooks (1990). "The Dance" (song): Written by Tony Arata. Label: Capitol Nashville.

About the Author

Born in 1959, Ken Horn is a first-generation American. He is the son of Joachim and Ursula who fled communist East Germany to come to America. The family was sponsored by a small Lutheran Church in Indian Village in Detroit, Michigan.

He currently lives in Frankenmuth, Michigan, where he met his wife, Veronica. They have two children, Kevin and Andrea.

Kevin and his wife, Ruth, also live with them in Frankenmuth and have blessed "Oma and Opa" with three beautiful grandchildren: Liam, Zellie who is terribly missed, and Zellie's little sister, Aaliyah.

Elected in 1992, Ken was a Saginaw County commissioner for fourteen years, then served in the Michigan House of Representatives for six years. Now in his second term in the Michigan Senate, Ken is Chairman of the Senate Economic Development committee. His legislative priorities include economic development, energy issues, education, and workforce development. Ken was deeply involved in the Midwest Council of State Governments and was elected to be Chairman of the Midwest Legislative Conference in 2020.

Ken holds a bachelor's degree in criminal justice from Concordia University in Ann Arbor. He earned his black belt in 2005, after training and teaching with the American Tae Kwon Do Academy. Ken is involved in many local civic groups and charities.

As an amateur writer, Ken has written unpublished poetry and published trade journal articles, news editorials, and officeholder newsletters. This first new book, *Letters to Heaven*, transformed his writing from a hobby to a labor of love.

CPSIA information can be obtained
at www.ICGtesting.com
Printed in the USA
JSHW060301170922
30643JS00003B/9